DYNASTY

The Authorized Biography of the Carringtons

INTRODUCTION BY

Esther Shapiro

A DOLPHIN BOOK

DOUBLEDAY & COMPANY, INC., GARDEN CITY, NEW YORK 1984

Library of Congress Cataloging in Publication Data
Main entry under title:
Dynasty: the authorized biography of the Carringtons.
    1. Dynasty (Television program)   I. Shapiro, Esther.
II. Dynasty (Television Program)
PN1992.77.D9D96   1984   791.45′72   84-10220
ISBN 0-385-19725-X
ISBN 0-385-19525-7 (pbk. Dolphin)

Manufactured in the United States of America
First Edition

Designed by Judith Neuman

PHOTOGRAPHY CREDITS

Larry Barbier, pp. 14, 24 (left), 25 (bottom), 41 (bottom), 42 (bottom right), 43, 49, 64, 80, 81, 84 (bottom), 94, 103 (top right), 115 (top), 122 (bottom right), 146–50; color insert #3—plate 8 (bottom).
Ron Batzdorff, pp. 27, 30 (top), 79 (bottom).
Jim Britt, pp. 15, 63, 115 (bottom left).
Bob Coburn, pp. 61, 103 (bottom right), 108.
Bob D'Amico, pp. x, 28, 44, 48 (bottom), 50–51, 59, 66 (right), 72, 76, 78 (top), 91 (bottom), 98, 116 (bottom), 120; color insert #1—plates 1, 2, 4, 5, 6, 7; color insert #2—plates 1, 7 (bottom), 8; color insert #3—plates 1, 2, 3, 4, 5, 6, 8 (top).
Chic Donchin, pp. 7 (bottom left), 8, 9 (top and center), 13, 19, (top), 21–23, 25 (top), 26 (bottom), 30 (bottom), 31, 34 (bottom), 35–38, 41 (top), 42 (top and bottom left), 48 (top), 58, 62, 66 (left), 78 (center and bottom), 79 (top and center), 84 (top and center), 91 (top), 93 (bottom), 111 (top), 114 (bottom), 122 (top right), 123 (top), 124–26, 133, 134, 135 (bottom), 136–39, 141, 142 (top right and bottom left), 143–45; color insert #1—plate 3; color insert #3—plate 7.
Jim Globus, pp. 56, 100 (right), 116 (top), 128–32.
Lynn Hunton, color insert #2—plate 2.
Lee Green, pp. 57, 69 (left), 123 (center).
Carol Ivie, p. 106.
Carol McCullough, p. 4 (top and center).
W. Russel Ohlson, pp. 140, 142 (top left and bottom right).
Richard Robinson, pp. 11 (bottom), 47, 52, 71, 77 (top), 109 (bottom), 118 (bottom).
Peter Sorel, pp. 16, 26 (top), 70 (left), 82, 93 (top), 103 (top left), 110 (bottom); color insert #2—plate 3 (top).
Gene Stein, pp. 7 (top right), 9 (bottom), 11 (top and center), 12, 18, 24 (right), 26 (center), 32–33, 34 (top), 40, 46, 54, 60, 68, 74 (top), 77 (bottom), 90 (top), 100 (left), 101, 103 (bottom left), 115 (bottom right), 118 (top and center), 122 (bottom left), 135 (top and center).
Bruce Talamon, pp. 4 (bottom), 7 (bottom right), 19 (bottom), 90 (bottom), 109 (top), 110 (top), 112, 122 (top left).
Randy Tepper, pp. 3, 7 (top left), 67, 69 (right), 70 (right), 74 (bottom), 85, 95, 96, 97, 109 (center), 111 (bottom), 123 (bottom).
Lee Wiener, p. 114 (top).
Brigitte Wiltzer, p. 86; color insert #1—plate 8.
Jerry Wolfe, pp. 88, 89.

CONTENTS

INTRODUCTION

Watching what the Carringtons do on "Dynasty" has become a weekly ritual for more than one hundred million people throughout the world. Viewers in more than seventy countries watch alone or together with family, friends, or strangers in homes, restaurants, college dorms, and bars—wherever a television set can be found. People rearrange work schedules, card games, theater nights to be able to spend an evening with Blake Carrington and his friends.

In Italy, "Dynasty" is aired twice a week to help satiate the appetite of the Italian audience. "Dynasty"—or "The Denver Clan" as it is known there—is the biggest hit in German television history. In countries where "Dynasty" has been banned or taken off the air because it is considered too racy—or, in some cases, too politically disquieting—for the populace, cassette sales have soared. Recently in Oslo, Norway, an opulent "Dynasty" ball was held; eight hundred of the country's most socially prominent people came dressed as their favorite character in the show. Stars Linda Evans, John Forsythe, John James, and Joan Collins are mobbed wherever they go. By the end of 1984 Metromedia projects that "Dynasty" will be seen on one hundred networks throughout the free world.

And in America "Dynasty" has been number one with women of all ages everywhere it has played for as long as it has been on the air. It is the second most popular show with teenagers and the third with men. And the demographics are growing.

My husband Richard and I are asked often these days—by friends, by the press, by serious students of the media—what we think the phenomenal appeal of "Dynasty" is based on. Are we dealing here with a broadcasting happenstance, a fortunate confluence of elements? Or are there built-in and predictable—not to mention replicable—components at work?

Our answer is usually a shrug and a secret smile, as if to suggest that we know and we're just not telling.

We are obviously thrilled, as are our partners and the ABC network, that people around the world enjoy "Dynasty." The why of it we have been content to leave to the media phenomenologists and the examiners of the history of television. However, the time may have come to say out loud why we think "Dynasty" works.

Certainly the casting contributes immeasurably. John Forsythe, Linda Evans, and Joan Collins are stars of great personal magnetism. Audiences like to watch them.

And we are fortunate to be partnered with Aaron Spelling, who is the most creative and successful producer in all of television. Yet there seems to be more.

Maybe, finally, it all comes down to this: there was an abiding purpose when we set out, which was to write and produce something we would enjoy watching, a continuing story of a fascinating—and purposefully not typical—American family to which we, like an audience, could become addicted.

It was a radical departure for us. In the sixties and seventies we had written and produced gritty social dramas—*Sarah T.: Portrait of a Teenage Alcoholic; Intimate Strangers; Minstrel Man; The Cracker Factory*—films that were, we hoped, thematically important and reflective of that period of great turbulence; films that explored the new sexual morality, that dramatized the new freedom that men and women were grabbing for (sometimes at the expense of courtship and marriage); films that examined, often psychologically, the search for self and control of one's destiny. "Important," "sensitive," "illuminating," "real," "socially significant" were words that we searched for in reviews.

And yet, somehow, as the years passed, we began to yearn for something we remembered from the movies we grew up with in the forties: stories where the audience pulled for men and women to fall in love and walk off into the sunset holding hands; stories with characters who dreamed of, pursued, and found their romantic ideal. It was one of the things, simple but undeniable, that, in those innocent days before the ubiquity of television, brought people into the theaters. And held them there.

There seemed to be a renewed need for romance. Perhaps it had never left but was merely neglected in the necessary reevaluation of more complex times.

And so we set out to create the ultimate American fantasy family. It would be a larger-than-life family. Rich, powerful, glamorous, living in Denver, whose principal business is oil. It would own mega-corporations. A football team. Horses. Airplanes. Limousines and fine motorcars. The Carringtons would live in a forty-eight-room mansion. A majordomo would run the household.

The men would buy and sell empires. They would be men who would enjoy being men. But they would also wear tuxedos and drink champagne. They would give expensive gifts and send flowers. And tell women—without having to mumble or scratch—how much they loved them.

The women would be extraordinarily beautiful and they would wear the prettiest clothes imaginable. But they would not be window dressing. Not furniture for men to use, not doormats. And never victims. The women of "Dynasty" would have lives and purposes. They would engage men competitively in business and with equal passion in bed. They too would be strong and goal-oriented within the context of the show. Nor would we require them to pay the price often extracted of uppity females in our neo-Victorian electronic fiction: they would never have to sacrifice their femininity.

The head of this family would be Blake Carrington, an attractive—sometimes imperious—man who deals brilliantly in business but fights equally hard to communicate with his children and to keep his family united. Blake Carrington would be able to do, to say what most every man in the audience would like to do and say if he were strong enough, articulate enough, romantic enough.

We gave Blake two grown children who might have caused King Solomon to wish he had paid more attention at a family planning seminar.

Son Steven would be honest and brave and manly. And openly—if not exclusively—homosexual; not ashamed of it, not defensive about it. His search for his sexual identity is ongoing, as are his problems with his father, whose notions about gayness are less than liberational (a view we feel he would share with no small segment of our audience). It was our intention here to present both sides of a controversial subject as fairly and straightforwardly as the format would allow.

Daughter Fallon would have great beauty, and charm, wit, education, in short, everything that money can buy, and yet all of that money and priviledge would not have bought her (cliché aside) happiness. Her life, her liaisons, her marriage are a shambles.

Steven and Fallon's mother, when she rejoined the family she was forced by Blake to abandon, would be Alexis Carrington Colby, calculating and diabolical, who would swear, however speciously, to give up all her devious ways if Blake would only take her back. Should he fail to do that, Alexis would set out to destroy the Carrington empire.

We were frankly concerned at the onset, what with all the intrigue woven into the fabric of "Dynasty," about who our viewers would find to care for and identify with. However much women might wish to be as self-possessed or, in their secret hearts, as acquisitive as Alexis or as free-spirited as Fallon, would they watch week after week this mythic American enclave of super-rich, outrageous, controversial, and sometimes unsympathetic characters? A bridge was needed to lead the audience from the real world to the fantasy world of the Carringtons. That bridge was, it turned out, felicitously easy to come by; she almost created herself.

Her name would be Krystle Grant Jennings, Blake's secretary, whom he would wed in the opening episode. An American Aphrodite, good as she is beautiful, Krystle maintains an abiding, charming—sometimes infuriating—disregard for Blake's wealth and a disconcerting propensity for keeping her head screwed on straight in spite of the opulence she has married into. She would epitomize everything women want to be and men want to love.

It would be Blake Carrington's adoration of Krystle and young Jeff Colby's near worship of Fallon that would provide the audience with that long-neglected fantasy, the finding and nurturing of romantic love.

From the beginning the plan was for the show to grow and change through personal and business confrontations. As long as dangerous business rivals, former husbands, lost children, poor or forgotten relatives continued to emerge, some pretenders, some real, all wanting to cross the moat to the Carrington castle, the dynasty—and "Dynasty"—would flourish.

So . . . having gone on perhaps longer than I intended about their genesis, I would like now to introduce you—more likely reintroduce you—to some good and dear and close friends of mine—along with friends and enemies of theirs. The Family Carrington.

Esther Shapiro

Co-Creator
Beverly Hills, California
1984

I.
THE DYNASTY

BLAKE CARRINGTON

Anticipation of the day's challenges puts a spring in his step as he descends the staircase of his luxuriously appointed forty-eight-room mansion. As handsome as a movie star in his thousand-dollar Brioni suit, he shares a tender kiss with his startlingly beautiful wife, Krystle. He smiles broadly. He is a man completely at home in this world of his own creation.

The head butler hands him his briefcase with a precision bred of practice, and the door closes behind legendary oil tycoon Blake Carrington, the possessor of everything a man could want: good health, a large family, and a fortune estimated at $200 million.

Picking up the phone in his black stretch limousine, as he makes his way to the airport, he relays orders to the thirty-five-story white marble tower that is the international headquarters of his dominion, Denver-Carrington. While flying to Washington, D.C., on his private Lear jet to address a congressional committee, the vital Carrington reviews a summary of his holdings.

Though he bears the charm, grace, and demeanor of a man born wealthy, Blake Carrington was merely born to *be* wealthy. Self-educated and self-made, Carrington is, through his company, the owner of hundreds of oil wells and leases, refineries and other diversified holdings. He is known as an innovator, the first, for example, to research and obtain patents on cost-effective methods of oil extraction from shale. Lionized by the press, he is a decision-maker, one who wields real power and who shapes the corporate picture of America. Carrington is forceful, intelligent, and self-confident. And he is obsessively devoted to his work.

On his honeymoon with his
new bride, Krystle Jennings
Carrington, 1980.

Rather than work for money, Blake decided early on to make
money work for him. He *planned* on being an influential man
and, at one time, considered running for Congress. But business became his religion, finance his life's blood. He cultivated
the eye of the tiger, assuring himself that his future hung in the
balance every day. Never is he complacent; never is he timid.
His strength is renewed by the certainty that his instincts are
rarely, if ever, wrong. He has become a tireless general, commanding his resources to aim higher and accomplish more.
And his ideology has yielded business triumph after business
triumph.

Born in Pennsylvania and raised in working-class surround-
ings, Carrington learned early on what it meant to work hard. It
is a lesson he has never had the arrogance to forget. Determined to have it all, as a youngster he worked at any job that

paid well, including a stint as the best soda jerk at the local diner, Annie's Eats. Even then, pride and willfulness drove him to be the best, and those two traits have never left him. His father was a small-scale-venture capitalist who intermittently had money, sometimes from oil, from a small bank, or from various investments, and then would lose it. Blake learned from his father that one could always rebuild from financial loss.

World War II transplanted him to Brittany, where his first taste of Old World elegance and art made a lasting impression. His all-consuming drive to succeed delivered him to postwar Colorado, where he risked his modest savings as a wildcatter.

Blake and Krystle on the main stairway of the mansion, 1980.

Blake testifying at the Dinard trial, 1981. He would insist, even after he was found guilty of manslaughter, that he was innocent.

Krystle, Jeff, and Fallon hoping for the best at the Dinard trial.

Sixteen years after she seemingly abandoned her family, Alexis Morell Carrington reappeared in Denver in 1981, to testify against her former husband at the Dinard trial. Her testimony was the critical factor in Blake's conviction.

Working as a rigger by day, attending college by night, Blake learned the oil business from below the ground up. When his well came in, as he knew it would, he was willing to gamble his success, parlaying it into an empire. Time after time he risked all. He was and is fiercely committed to never being less than the winner of every game life throws his way.

He demonstrated his right to privilege by the wealth he amassed. Blake made myth as easily as he made money, and his reputation earned him the attention of the socially ambitious Alexis Morell, a very young and breathtaking English beauty. Schooled in art, society, and manners, her refinement was as attractive to him as his charisma and money were to her.

Their love bloomed and they married in 1954; Colbyco Oil magnate Cecil Colby was best man. Though Blake loved Alexis, building Denver-Carrington took up most of his time, leaving his teenage bride much to herself.

In 1955 they had their first child, Adam, and in 1956, their daughter Fallon. Then, in September of 1957, the Carringtons were dealt a devastating blow. Adam was kidnapped from his baby carriage in the park. Though the case was front-page news across the country, neither the baby nor the kidnapper were found. Grief-stricken, Blake vowed to spend more time at home, doting on his daughter Fallon. He and Alexis decided to try and forget Adam, to put their heartache to rest. But the kidnapping shook the very foundations of their marriage. Alexis believed that had Blake not called the police, their little boy would have been returned.

In an effort to start their life anew, Blake searched for the most beautiful home in the state of Colorado. He found it and the Carringtons settled on the 645-acre estate just outside of Denver. The mansion itself was, as a local wag described it, "What God would have bought if God had the money." This was a suitable home for Blake's dynasty, a new place to rebuild his family. Alexis gave birth to another son, Steven, in 1958.

Although his good intentions were to concentrate on his family, his resolve faded whenever Denver-Carrington called. Travel and business removed him too frequently from the home and family he loved. As the years passed, his wife Alexis did not share the excitement of their growing empire and her youth and self-absorption made her restless. Eventually, in 1965, she sought comfort outside her marriage. Blake caught her in flagrante delicto with his estate manager, Roger Grimes. Enraged, Blake attacked the man. In the fight that ensued, Grimes was crippled for life. Blake, shocked by what he had done, used his money to assuage his guilt. A generous settlement persuaded the former employee that he need not prosecute.

The incident caused Blake an irreversible change of heart where Alexis was concerned. The trust he had taken for granted was destroyed, his hopes for their future ruined, and the betrayal haunted him. Irredeemably soiled in his mind, Alexis, he thought, was an unfit mother for their children, one of whom was nine years old and the other nearly seven. Playing upon Alexis' own guilt, and their mutual desire to spare the children an ugly and sure-to-be-sensationalized custody battle, Blake persuaded Alexis to leave. With a $250,000-a-year trust fund to guarantee her well-being and the condition she never contact the children, Alexis was exiled from Blake's Garden of Eden.

The experience hardened Blake. It was the first time in his life he had lost. Stunned by this realization, he plunged even more heartily into the one success he was sure of—his work. It drew him closer to his daughter Fallon, who seemed to understand and faithfully adored him. It alienated him from his son Steven, who craved the lavish affection that his mother had always given him, and which Blake could not find in his heart. Steven had been Alexis' favorite.

Denver-Carrington continued to grow and prosper under Blake's sure hand. Soon he was rich as Croesus, ready and willing to indulge his young children. His caveat: aim high and always get what you aim for. He struggled to instill this philosophy in his children. He expected Carringtons to possess his ambition and dash, to compete and *win*. Fallon was receptive, Steven was not. Blake believed his family was the reward for his long hours of hard work. He would do, and had done, whatever was necessary to ensure their happiness and safety— to the best of his ability.

In what little spare time he had, Blake began recreational activities to relieve stress and stay fit. He became an expert horseman, an expert swimmer, and an exceptional opponent in tennis and pool.

Through these years, Blake cultivated the fairer sex only as a social necessity. He dated many beautiful and desirable women, but he could not bring himself to trust any of them. Then he met the ravishing Krystle Jennings. Taken by her natural beauty, her clear eyes, lack of pretension, and softspoken honesty, he hired her as his secretary. To be around her made him happy. He came to cherish her, *trust* her. She was the one luxury that would complete his life—the center jewel his crown had always lacked.

In his customary style of going after what he wanted, Blake pursued Krystle. She was overwhelmed by his immense wealth and intimidated by his strong resolve. She was as unsure as he was dead certain. For him, his frequent gifts of flowers and jew-

ABOVE Much to Blake's dismay, Alexis moved into the estate art studio in 1981 She still held deed to it from the early 1960s.

BELOW With the fear that Steven might suffer brain damage from a fall in 1981, Blake comforts Alexis at Denver Memorial Hospital. It is a rare moment, one that reminds them of the past they once shared as husband and wife, and as parents of their children.

ABOVE Three newspapers are delivered every morning to Blake at breakfast: *The Denver Chronicle*, *The Wall Street Journal*, and *The New York Times*.

BELOW Blake describes himself as "a high roller."

Temporarily blinded by a bomb blast in 1981, Blake listens as Joseph reads a card from Logan Rhinewood, the mobster responsible. He sent Blake a white cane as a present.

els were manifestations of his love; for her, they were pressure. She backed off. In time he won, and she realized she loved him as much as he loved her.

They were married on May 24, 1980, and the wedding in the ballroom at the mansion was the loving fulfillment of Blake's dreams. It seemed to Blake an augur that the decade of the eighties would be his best. It also marked the reunion of his family: Fallon returned from her meanderings abroad and Steven returned from New York City. But the reunion was less

Wanting to avenge his brother's death, for which he incorrectly blamed Blake, Nick Toscanni attacked Blake on a trail in the Rockies, 1982. Blake won the fight, but then a rattlesnake scared Blake's horse, which threw him and knocked him out. Nick left him there to die; Krystle found him and got him to the hospital.

Krystle embraces Blake in the hospital, helping him toward a speedy recovery after the Toscanni incident.

than joyous. Fallon's jealousy flared; she was openly hostile to Krystle. And Blake's suspicion of Steven's homosexuality was confirmed.

Blake and Krystle's honeymoon included visits to Hawaii, Tahiti, and Samoa, but it was cut short by a crisis involving Blake's oil tankers in the Middle East. The honeymoon was over. Soon business pressures and familial strife set Blake on an uncharacteristic bout of drinking. Arguments with Steven accelerated. When Blake unexpectedly found him embracing his former lover, Ted Dinard, on the night of November 12, blind rage overtook him. He lunged at the man and Dinard fell, hit his head, and died.

The decade that had started so fortuitously only months before bore the nadir of Blake's life: his trial for manslaughter. The sensational murder trial was rocked by a surprise witness: a vengeful Alexis. Her testimony contributed to his conviction. His sentence was two years' probation.

The outcome of the trial caused Cecil Colby to call in an outstanding loan, and Blake, on the brink of ruin, was forced to fly to Las Vegas where he traded 45 percent interest in his football team for the $9 million cash he needed. Kingpin Logan Rhinewood (whom no one had ever seen) seemed an odd business partner for Blake, but he himself has admitted, "I've gone to congressmen and kings and dictators and mob bosses when I needed help—and I got it." It was not a good partnership. When Blake blocked Rhinewood's interference with the team, Blake was blinded by a bomb blast in the stadium parking lot in 1981. Using his influence in Washington, Blake initiated a crime commission investigation into Rhinewood. During the course of the hearing, Blake regained his sight, but the elusive Rhinewood got off the hook.

In 1982, Blake was horrified to learn that Cecil Colby was, in fact, Rhinewood. Colby, embittered by business and personal reasons, found his final revenge on Blake by marrying Alexis. His death bestowed on her the wealth and power of Colbyco, and his will also left instructions for her to destroy Blake in any way she could.

In 1983 Krystle discovered that her divorce from her first husband was a fraud, leaving her marriage to Blake invalid. A series of misunderstandings between her and Blake caused them to separate, and Krystle moved into Fallon's hotel, La Mirage. Although family problems continued to plague Blake, Fallon and Steven each presented a grandson to him. The guaranteed continuation of his dynasty cheered Blake tremendously. But, in 1983, when Steven's marriage to Sammy Jo Dean broke up and a gay lawyer was subsequently living in Steven's apartment, Blake sued for custody of Steven Daniel Carrington,

Blake gives a loving welcome to his first grandson, Blake Carrington Colby, 1982. He was the greatest gift Fallon could give her father.

Blake, Krystle and little Blake.

Meeting his son Adam, 1982, in his office at Denver-Carrington.

Blake meets his second grandson, Steven Daniel Carrington, Jr., 1983.

Jr. It was a bitter hearing that divided the family and further estranged Blake and Krystle. Although the court dismissed the case when Steven married Claudia Blaisdel, the conflict between father and son was not completely resolved.

In a final coup to Blake's trials and tribulations of 1983, Alexis very nearly succeeded in a takeover of Denver-Carrington by Colbyco. The only positive event during the first part of the year (and that was debatable at times) was the return of Blake's long-lost son Adam. Then something truly wonderful did happen: Blake and Krystle were remarried in a joyous ceremony in the Carrington home.

Nineteen eighty-four has been a year of highs and lows. The

Blake intercepted by reporters on his way to court, 1983. Outraged that Chris Deegan was living with Steven and Danny, and assuming incorrectly that Steven and Chris were lovers, Blake sued for custody of Danny.

high was Krystle's much-prayed-for conception of another child; the low was Blake's loss of $100 million in a double cross on a China Sea oil-lease deal with Rashid Ahmed. Though the Carringtons' personal future looks bright, the fortune that vaulted them into the spotlight of the world may indeed be lost.

Blake may ponder the setbacks he will next confront, but he is secure in the knowledge that he will meet the challenges head-on and remain the winner he has made himself. But should he fail in some way, should he die, the dynasty he has worked so long and so hard for will continue on—in the Carrington family.

Blake found the body of his close friend and Carrington majordomo, Joseph Anders, after he committed suicide in 1983. Blake assumed personal responsibility for Joseph's daughter, Kirby, and has treated her as a member of the family.

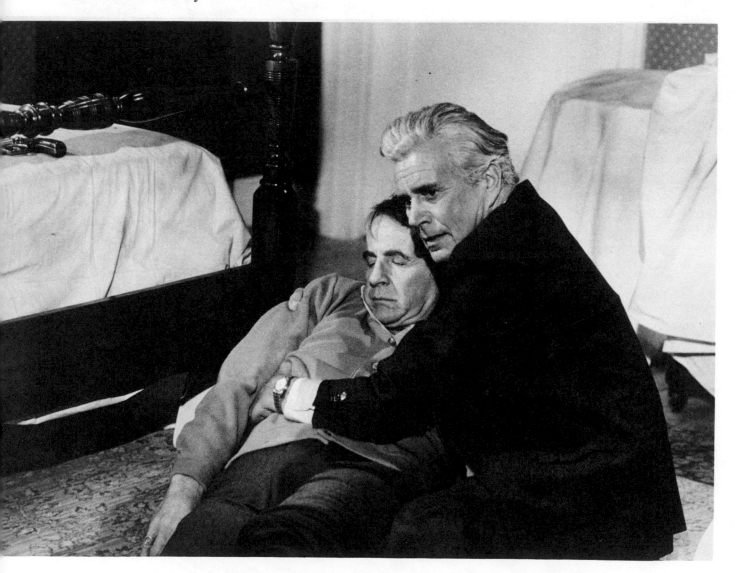

Most often seen in a suit and
tie, Blake here is casual and
at-home—a Blake rarely seen
by outsiders.

KRYSTLE CARRINGTON

Her story is straight out of a fairy tale. Krystle Jennings, a shy divorcée in her mid thirties, was a humble secretary in an oil field office, typing drilling reports and feeding a Xerox machine. Blake Carrington, extremely debonaire, handsome and prosperous, was immediately taken with her exquisite face, soft smile, and gentle ways. She became Blake's personal secretary. Soon after, the search he had been on for most of his life was over. But Krystle, overwhelmed by his riches and lavish attentions, was not quite sure. Although she had abandoned the concept decades before, she came to realize Blake was indeed her Prince Charming. The slipper fit, and their wedding took place on May 24, 1980.

"Happily ever after" has had its ups and downs, but their love for each other has ultimately flourished. Knowing Krystle, it is hard to imagine how it could be otherwise. Good-natured and effervescent, she lights up every room she enters. Under Blake's loving support, she has blossomed to fulfill the promise of her natural grace and ease. Her warmth, sincerity, and wit have endeared her to Blake's world. Perhaps her most outstanding feature is her ability to remain calm in a crisis, an asset required almost daily in the Carrington clan.

Krystle Grant was born of working-class parents in an Ohio town that she described to Blake as "smaller than your dining room." When her father died, he didn't leave his family two hundred dollars to bury him. (No wonder, then, that she was unworldly, especially in the Carrington world of high style, high society, high finance, and not-so-high morality.) Krystle married rising tennis star Samuel Mark Jennings (Mark) and they moved to nearby Dayton, Ohio.

Mark's tennis tournaments took him out of town for weeks at a time. He made a successful start professionally, but what had

Krystle's affair with Matthew Blaisdel came very close to resuming in 1980, at a time when she and Blake were experiencing marital problems, but she refrained, realizing how deeply she loved Blake.

An expectant Krystle shows Blake her first present for the baby. She wanted to make sure the child was, indeed, "born with a silver spoon in his mouth." Her miscarriage was to torment Krystle until 1984, when she conceived again.

been "promise" soured quickly in the cutthroat arena of pro tennis. The defeat invaded their marriage. Mark's circuit sponsor suddenly dropped him after Mark double-faulted away a crucial match at La Costa. The failure netted another double fault—the end of his tennis career and the end of their marriage. Despite their mutual love for one another, Mark again took to the road, this time for a divorce in Guadalajara, Mexico.

Described as "basically a shut-up-and-keep-swimming kind of lady," Krystle took her sixty-words-a-minute typing skills and swam West. In an interview with Blake Carrington, he asked her what, aside from getting a job at the prestigious Denver-Carrington, was most important to her. Krystle answered, "Life. Living life to the fullest." That was the freestyle stroke that landed her the job that landed her the Prince.

Just prior to working for Blake, Krystle had an affair with Denver-Carrington oil-field geologist Matthew Blaisdel. A married man, Matthew left for a more lucrative job in the company's Middle East fields to help pay his wife Claudia's enormous sanatorium costs. Krystle knew he was married and had a daughter, but their attraction, their mutual loneliness, had launched the love affair. His departure seemed the only way to end it, and the guilt.

Krystle's marriage to Blake took place in his magnificent mansion. Last-minute preparations included Krystle's signing a premarital agreement presented by Blake's lawyer, Andrew Laird.

Their honeymoon to Hawaii, Tahiti, and Samoa had them basking in the sensual splendor of the tropics before a crisis at Denver-Carrington cut it short. Threatened by financial trouble with his interests overseas, Blake named Krystle to his corporate board and put all of his assets in her name. The expedient

RIGHT Krystle greets her niece and future stepdaughter-in-law, Sammy Jo Dean. Her blindness to Sammy Jo's true character stemmed from Krystle's deep love for her dead sister, Iris.

BELOW Nick Toscanni with Krystle in her bedroom after the riding "accident" that caused the miscarriage of her unborn child. After her physical recovery, Blake hired him to treat Krystle for her subsequent depression, unaware of the fact that Nick had fallen in love with her, while at the same time carrying on an affair with Fallon.

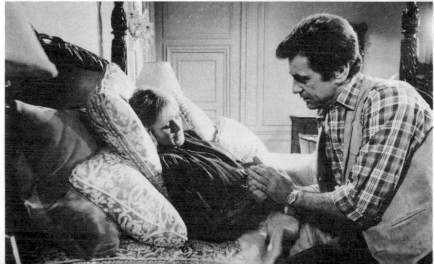

maneuver was intended to protect his net worth from his creditors, but it piqued Krystle's interest in his business dealings. She knew how much of Blake was in his business and she wanted to share that. Blake, however, didn't want to involve her further in his business because he wanted Krystle to have his child.

Respecting his wishes, Krystle dived headlong into her new role as mistress of the manor. At first, she wished that Blake would send her to school, to learn "how to be rich and happy while a guest in his own home." What she didn't realize then was her capacity to learn all that and more. She knew nothing of French furniture, managing servants, or social etiquette (as Blake's daughter Fallon was only too happy to remind her), but her willingness to learn and the support of Blake led her to an understanding of finery and an ease with wealth.

An immediate rapport with Blake's son Steven softened the blow of Fallon's initial contempt. Even-headed about money, Krystle always believed that heart and hearth provided more comfort than bank accounts. Her first months at the mansion confirmed that belief. Krystle had always been a family person, but she had never encountered a family like this. The family had an abundance of everything, including, unfortunately, anger, jealousy, and resentment.

Those first months also plagued her with doubts about Blake himself. Krystle wondered whether she had reached too high, that perhaps she belonged with the more mortal Matthew, who had returned to Denver. She narrowly resisted resuming the affair, but when Matthew resigned from Denver-Carrington to strike out on his own and critically needed money, Krystle did pawn an emerald necklace Blake had given her to bail him out.

There was a series of problems in the family, and pressure from Blake to have a child (which she felt was premature until things settled down) mounted. Krystle, not normally deceptive, took birth control pills, feeling uncomfortable and lost in what was beginning to seem like a double life. When a drunken Blake violently confronted her about the pills, Krystle decided to leave to sort things out. However, when she learned of Blake's trial for manslaughter in the death of Steven's former lover, Ted Dinard, Krystle dutifully returned to the side of the man she loved.

During the trial, a board meeting at Denver-Carrington was called in an attempt to unseat Blake. Krystle, as Executive Vice President, attended in Blake's absence. Her staunch defense of Blake was delivered with a rhetorical brilliance that surprised even her. She successfully postponed any action by the board until Blake's return. Krystle got her first savored taste of power.

In 1981, an elated Krystle conceived her first child, but a tragic accident while horseback riding resulted in an emotional-

20

ly devastating miscarriage. Her suspicions that Blake's former wife, Alexis, had deliberately caused it, created a deep-seated hatred for Alexis that evoked violence from her otherwise gentle nature.

After the miscarriage, Krystle remained in a state of depression. Blake hired Dr. Nick Toscanni to treat her. Toscanni quickly fell in love with her, but despite problems in her marriage, Krystle resisted him.

Her troubles were far from over. In 1982, she tried to take a gun away from the mentally unstable Claudia Blaisdel and it went off. Claudia was hit in the side of the head. Police investigators learned of Krystle's past affair with Claudia's husband, Matthew, and interpreted it as a motive for Krystle to shoot Claudia. Under suspicion of attempted murder, Krystle was unnerved and helpless until Claudia finally vindicated her by confessing that she had pulled the trigger herself.

Later that year, Krystle was shocked to learn that her divorce

Krystle storming Alexis' art studio on the estate with the evidence in hand—Alexis' rifle. After putting the clues together, Krystle accused her of purposely firing the rifle to scare her horse and subsequently causing her miscarriage. Their confrontation resulted in a vicious fight that nearly destroyed the interior of the studio in 1982. (OVER)

21

from Mark Jennings was merely a piece of paper he purchased in a Mexican bar. With her marriage to Blake invalid, Krystle left the turmoil of their relationship to think things over at Fallon's nearby hotel, La Mirage. Blake's emotional self-sufficiency, Alexis' continual interference, and the myriad chaos of Carrington alliances and vendettas gave her a lot to think about. Her confusion was compounded by Mark's being hired as the tennis pro at La Mirage. Krystle wrestled with her old ties of love with Mark, but she proceeded with a legal divorce.

While Krystle and Blake were still estranged, Alexis seized the moment and, at Steven Carrington's cabin, offered her one million dollars to leave Blake for good. Krystle was outraged. When she tried to leave, she found the door bolted shut and the cabin in flames. The two women were nearly killed before they were rescued by Mark Jennings.

When Krystle's divorce from Mark became final, Krystle decided she needed a change in her life. In 1983 she joined Denver-Carrington as Chief of Public Relations. Energetic, quick, personable, Krystle succeeded brilliantly in the job, and it gave her a new sense of confidence. It also gave her a chance to get to know Blake all over again, and they remarried the same year.

In 1984, Krystle conceived again and Blake celebrated her pregnancy by giving her a sable coat, a diamond bracelet, and a

ABOVE Krystle and her first husband, tennis pro Mark Jennings, in the early 1970s.

RIGHT Krystle and Alexis run into one another at the costumers in preparation for the Roaring Twenties Ball, 1982. Krystle won a coin toss and Alexis had to wear something else.

new car and chauffeur. The money for these gifts, however, spent so freely as a matter of habit, may be desperately needed by the Carringtons. But even if the Carrington fortune is lost, Krystle is a woman who wants her husband more than anything else, for richer or for poorer.

It pleases Krystle to at long last share the frustrations and challenges of Blake's life. She still greets each day with bright-eyed vitality and a zest for living. Her goodness and concern for others are stabilizing factors in the Carrington family, ones that have earned her the admiration and respect of all. Krystle Carrington is a tender, loving, feminine woman—a passionate romantic living the life of every girl's dream, but bringing to it common sense, compassion, and cachet. She is truly a beautiful human being.

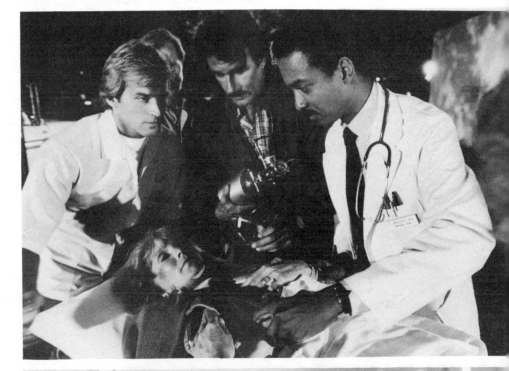

A worried Mark Jennings oversees Krystle's medical care following her rescue from the burning cabin, 1983. Passionately in love with her since they were married, he made his final attempt to win her back. He was unsuccessful.

Krystle hugs Blake in Memorial Hospital after she was caught in Steven's burning cabin, 1983. Their estrangement would continue over Blake's suspicions that Mark was the attempted killer.

Krystle told Blake, "You're like a man on a mountain sometimes, Blake, your mountain—and you don't want anyone to climb it with you."

Krystle with her grandson Danny. She and Blake were in the process of adopting him when Steven returned from Singapore in 1983. She loves him as if he were her own son.

Blake and Krystle having lunch at La Mirage, 1983. Their attempt at reconciliation blew up over Blake's trying to gain custody of Danny.

Krystle in a pensive moment. Despite all of the people living in the mansion, it can sometimes be a very lonely place.

ALEXIS CARRINGTON COLBY

She exudes an aura of sensuality and sophistication. Her breathtaking jewels are worth a king's ransom; her personal couturier keeps her on the world's best-dressed list; her elegant penthouse is incomparable. Alexis Carrington Colby is a fearless, intelligent, independent dynamo who simply never settles for less than the very best, a world-class woman who is totally in control of her life, who never goes anywhere without being the center of attention . . . and she knows it.

A jet setter with important connections in government, society, finance, and fashion, Alexis is also a talented painter, equally skilled in still life and in portraiture. Her sense of color, design, and style pervade her every nuance. She is an arbiter of taste wherever she goes; she is conversant in art, ballet, and theater, and speaks fluent French, Spanish, and Italian. Never happy with another's ideas, she brands everything she touches with her distinctive signature . . . including men.

Her legion of conquests include men of every nationality, from capitals of the world to playgrounds of the rich and famous. Her inviting lips, fiery eyes, and voluptuous figure are only the visible temptations few men can resist. A femme fatale who is all too aware of where her power lies, Alexis has charmed captains and kings, diplomats and dilettantes. Captivating, alluring, and unquestionably a vamp, Alexis is the personification of Kipling's observation that the female of the species is deadlier than the male.

Born in England on the eve of World War II, Alexis Morell was stubbornly persistent, even as a child. After her father's death, her mother reputedly developed a taste for men who played hard to get—a taste her daughter appears to have inherited. Alexis attended a boarding school in Switzerland (and was expelled), briefly worked as an artist's model in Brussels, then entered the Royal Academy of Dramatic Art for one year. (She majored, one would have to suppose, in dramatic entrances.)

29

Krystle once observed about Alexis, "You either love her or hate her. And she seems to enjoy it either way."

Alexis and Cecil Colby making their entrance at the party at the mansion held in honor of Steven and Sammy Jo, 1982. A year after she married Blake, when she was eighteen, Alexis had had a brief affair with Cecil. More than twenty-five years later, they resumed their passion.

Alexis and Steven in his apartment, 1981. Alexis: "I wanted to cook something for you tonight. A home-cooked meal . . . so I catered this from Jensen's."

At seventeen, she married rising entrepreneur Blake Carrington who was about to launch the Carrington name into the highest financial and social circles.

After their marriage, Blake's increasing business demands, as he amassed his fortune, left her on her own far too much of the time. After the birth of their first child, Adam, in 1955, restless, bored, and unwilling to languish on the sidelines as her husband's acclaim and fortunes grew, she had a brief affair with Blake's best friend, Cecil Colby. Feeling guilty, still passionately in love with Blake, she resolved to be a good wife. In 1956, she gave birth to a daughter, Fallon.

The kidnapping of Adam in 1957 left Alexis bereft and even more disconnected. She tried to suppress her restlessness by attending to the new mansion, bearing another son, Steven, in 1958, rearing the children, and pursuing her painting.

Her collaborative effort with estate manager Roger Grimes in building an art studio on the grounds led her into an affair. When Blake found them in bed together in 1965, and Alexis saw Blake violently confront and beat Grimes with an insane passion, she knew fear for the first time in her life. Aggravated

31

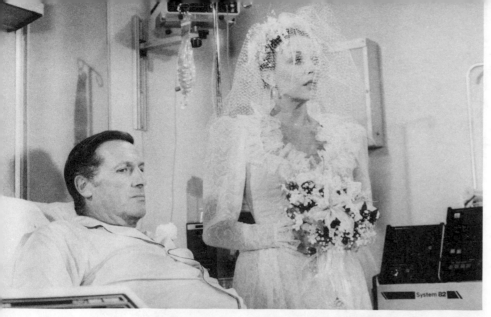

The unusual but necessary wedding ceremony of Alexis Morell Carrington to Cecil Colby, in the intensive care unit of Denver Memorial Hospital, 1982.

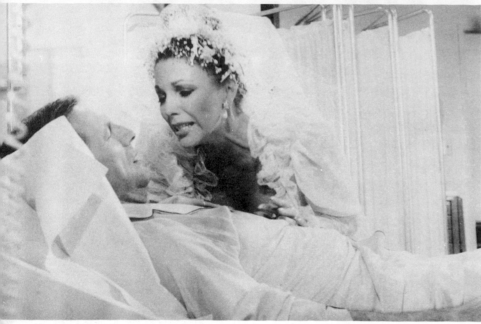

Alexis watches in horror as her new husband suffers another heart attack.

by her extreme sense of guilt, and accepting Blake's accusation that she was an unfit mother, she agreed to leave quietly.

Living on the $250,000-a-year trust fund Blake established to comfort her in her banishment, Alexis took up residence in the jet-set capital of Acapulco. She found agreeable amusement in the company of playboys, beachboys, and bellboys. The pain she suffered over the loss of her children subsided only when she traveled to new places. Capri, Portofino, and Cannes were only a few of the ports of call on her international itinerary.

Alexis' dramatic return to Denver, as the surprise witness in the 1981 manslaughter trial of Blake Carrington, stunned her ex-husband and children. Her unanticipated testimony about Blake's alleged violent past fanned the flames of an already overpublicized courtroom drama.

Seeing Blake again overcame Alexis' hatred, and her love for him was rekindled brighter, more desperately, than ever before.

Alexis anxiously awaits the fate of her husband.

The bereaved widow, Mrs. Cecil Colby.

ABOVE A guilt-ridden Alexis tries to whisk Jeff out of Memorial Hospital to Switzerland. Blake stopped her. Alexis has adored Jeff since he was a little boy and while she knew of Adam's plot to confuse his mind, she had no idea it would almost kill him in 1983.

LEFT Alexis, like everyone else (except Blake), had given Steven up for dead. Grief such as she had never felt before had torn through her, and the return of her favorite child instilled in her a sense of gratitude she had never previously experienced. 1983.

(OVER) Little did Alexis know Krystle's state of mind this day in 1983, else she would have steered clear of her. (Their fight in Alexis' studio in 1982 taught her that Krystle's temper—though rarely ignited—made her a particularly dangerous opponent.) Krystle had been agonizing over the departure of little Danny from the mansion when Alexis stopped by to make false accusations that Krystle was trying to turn Fallon against her. And bam! The ladies were off until Blake broke up the fight. To Alexis' delight, Blake humiliated Krystle in front of her.

After all her world travels, after all her affairs, Blake was and is to this day the single thing she wants most in life. He is the only man she's ever known who is as strong and willful as she is. Following Blake's conviction, Alexis stayed on in Denver, determined to steal him back from Krystle. When her advances were spurned, the pain of rejection made her turn her energy toward the one action she instinctively knew how to use—*revenge.*

Retaliation while retrieving the affection of her children proved to be tricky business. Alexis moved into the art studio on the estate (she still held deed to it) and set about disrupting Blake's family life. She relished her success, but her treachery invariably affected Fallon and Steven. Her renewed relationship with them was rocky, one that alternately elated and grieved her.

Alexis made an unexpectedly powerful enemy in Krystle. She grossly underestimated her rival until she experienced the sting of steel that lay beneath Krystle's gentle looks. Her nemesis, Krystle, would cause Alexis frustration, envy, and hatred for years to come.

In 1982, Alexis married Blake's arch business rival and former friend, Cecil Colby, while he was in the hospital recovering from a heart attack. Cecil suffered another one during the ceremony and, just as it seemed he might recover, died. Because Cecil and Blake had had a severe falling-out the year before, he left Alexis one of the richest women in the world, with controlling interest in Colbyco and instructions to destroy Blake.

The legacy from Colby made Alexis a powerful business foe for Blake to contend with. Alexis was determined to overtake Denver-Carrington and thus gain control over Blake and his dy-

nasty. She nearly succeeded in 1983, but her maternal love for Adam forced her to call off the merger in order to protect him.

As the Chairman of the Board of Colbyco, Alexis has been the sole woman to break the male domination of the oil business. Her commanding presence and her leadership abilities have brought the international company to new heights. Her business associates, even her adversaries, declare her a brilliant corporate executive. Alexis savors competition, and, though she acknowledges that winning does have its rewards, it is the race itself that most invigorates her. She has been accused, from time to time, of unbridled ruthlessness, but while she will do whatever it takes to gain her objective, she occasionally displays a sense of fair play that allows her to make it up later to anyone who may innocently have fallen casualty to the battle. A proud beauty and a formidable force, Alexis has a never-ending thirst for novelty which billion-dollar corporate business sates from time to time.

At first glance, Alexis Carrington Colby may appear tempestuous and unpredictable; those who know her well recognize the cold calculation that lies beneath the illusion of caprice. She is determined to get what she wants and will stop at nothing. Alexis possesses a combination of savvy and smoldering sexuality that keeps both friends and enemies on constant guard. While certainly not without her peccadilloes, she is not the piranha some have claimed. Underneath it all, she is a woman capable of great love, whose devotion to her children can result in a fierce protectiveness, which in turn is often misinterpreted as cold brutality. Her toughened and guarded façade is merely armor for a core of vulnerability that lies deep within her.

Still, she is an inveterate schemer—one who is never very far away from the cause of pending disaster. She likes to be the carrier of news, especially when it is bad. She has been the target for many. In 1983, for example, the Carrington's major-domo, Joseph Anders, tried to burn her to death in Steven's cabin, and later he tried to smother her with a pillow in the hospital. If Alexis does indeed, as many have claimed, have nine lives, she is guarding the remaining ones carefully. She employed her former lover, Mark Jennings, as a full-time bodyguard. But in an ironic twist of fate, Alexis was arrested in 1984 as *his* suspected murderer.

A talked-about woman wherever she goes, Alexis has accomplished more, lost more, fought back harder, and simply *lived* more than scores of her feminine counterparts (Cleopatra, Catherine the Great, et al.). A determined woman if there ever was one, if there is any way for her to win Blake back, she will find it. And she won't give up until she does, or dies.

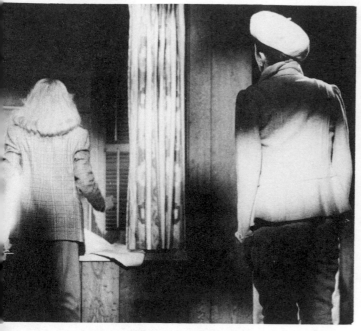

Alexis and Krystle caught in the deliberately set fire in Steven's cabin, 1983. The cabin doors were bolted shut from the outside and they would have died had Mark Jennings not appeared.

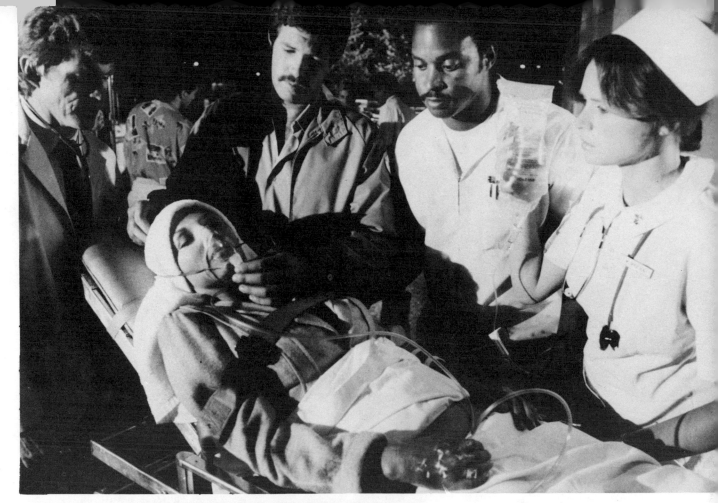

ABOVE Alexis was rushed to the hospital.

LEFT Though she suffered head wounds and burns, Alexis' classic beauty still radiates during her hospital stay following the fire.

In 1983, Alexis hired Mark Jennings to be her bodyguard. There was no longer any romance between them. (Jennings died tragically in 1984, from a fall from the balcony of Alexis' penthouse apartment.)

BELOW On a business trip with Dex in 1983, Alexis cut loose in a country-western bar. A superb dancer, Alexis mesmerized the entire place. She also sang that night: "See What the Boys in the Back Room Will Have."

BELOW After double-crossing her in business, Deke Dexter, "Dex," began a passionate affair with the older Alexis in 1983.

Alexis accepting a gift from the powerful Middle East tycoon, Rashid Ahmed, with whom she once had an affair. In 1984, Alexis convinced him to double-cross Blake in a major oil-leasing deal, but she lost Dex in the process when he caught her with Ahmed the next morning in a compromising position.

ADAM CARRINGTON

There is a revenge fantasy common among poor and pow-
erless boys that one day their *true* identity will be pro-
claimed and it will be revealed that they are the long-lost
heir of a tremendously wealthy and powerful family. *Then* their
transgressors will be sorry. At the least, they will be forced to
treat them with the deferential respect due them all along. Michael Torrance reveled in that fantasy more than once and, in
1982, was shocked to learn that the fantasy was the truth: he
was a long-lost heir, he *was* rich and powerful.

This is how the discovery came about:

Blake Carrington went on national television to plead for the
return of his kidnapped grandson, little Blake. Alexis Carrington Colby joined in, dramatically retelling the story of their eldest son's kidnapping twenty-five years earlier. Kate Torrance,
whom Michael thought was his grandmother, saw the broadcast and, on her deathbed, told him that he was the missing
Carrington baby.

Kate's son, David Torrance, and his wife had a son, but all
three had died in a car crash. Kate, hysterical with grief, saw a
pretty baby boy lying in a carriage in a Denver park. She stole
the baby, brought him back to a ranch in Billings, Montana,
where she raised him, telling him that he had survived the car
crash that killed his parents.

Kate's dying wish was that Michael rejoin his true family.
She presented him with a tiny sterling-silver rattle, mono-
grammed with the initials A.A.C., to verify her tale. It had been
in the carriage with him.

Armed with his key to the kingdom, Michael flew to Denver
and presented himself to his father, Blake Carrington. Dismiss-
ing him as a pretender to the throne, Blake promptly ejected
Michael from his office. It wasn't so much that Blake didn't
want to believe that Michael was his son, he was just *scared* to

entertain the hope. Even twenty-five years later, the pain of their son's disappearance was still very much alive for both Blake and Alexis. Michael then approached Alexis, proffering the rattle. When the original jeweler confirmed the rattle's serial number to Alexis, Adam's stake was claimed.

So, without so much as pulling sword from stone, Adam Alexander Carrington assumed his birthright—heir apparent to the Carrington empire.

As a boy, Adam was alone much of the time. Kate never allowed him to go on school trips or play with other children. His emotional vulnerability was compounded by a nervous breakdown in high school, resulting from his experimentation with psychedelic drugs. It had taken months to nurse him back to mental health, and the attending doctor feared that he had not been as successful as he had hoped. Adam would be haunted by his youthful experimentation for the rest of his life.

Adam worked his way through Yale by waiting on children of the rich in campus dining rooms. Kate, who always hoped he would be a state senator, mortgaged the ranch to finance the Yale law degree she expected would be his ticket.

Now that Adam had reclaimed his birthright, he was not about to let it go, not even for a second. In a matter of days he switched from beer to brandy, quickly acquiring a taste for the finest. With his jaw set, he was determined to become one of them. But he baffled his new family; he was alternately shy and loving, then hostile and defiant. He was an angry young man, but one who tried very hard to fit in.

Bearing the imperiousness of Alexis and the ambition of Blake, he was viewed by everyone, except his parents, as a treacherous young turk. Perhaps Blake and Alexis instinctively

Blake and Alexis make a televised plea to the kidnapper to return little Blake, 1982. This crisis dredged up the horror of the kidnapping of their first son, Adam, in 1957—the crisis that started the alienation between them so many years before. The broadcast led to Adam's discovering his true identity.

knew a secret side of the man—a man who was emotionally isolated, fearful of rejection, and who desperately wanted to love and be loved by the family he never had. Unfortunately, Adam lacked the skill and the patience to communicate his needs.

When Blake belatedly recognized Adam as his son and offered him a job at Denver-Carrington, Adam avenged his hurt by throwing the offer back in his face and announcing his new position with Alexis at Colbyco. He was anxious to reward his mother for being the first to embrace him.

Adam initially did not fare well with his sister, either. Before their true link was known to them, Adam had met Fallon while he was staying at La Mirage. The two of them were instantly attracted to one another; at one point they kissed. They intended to pursue a romantic involvement but discovered they were brother and sister. Adam's mistake was not the incident itself, since neither of them had known; his mistake was, when Fallon refused to welcome him into the family with open arms, punishing her by reminding her of their initial sexual attraction. Fallon resented and mistrusted him for a long time afterward.

Adam seems to have inherited his mother's emotional philosophy (a "you-hurt-me-and-I'll-kill-you" attitude) to a severe degree. For example, Adam fell in love with Kirby Anders at first sight. When she rejected his advances, he raped her. He continued chasing her, trying to woo her with a combination of love, warmth, and violent threats, even after her marriage to Jeff Colby.

Adam showed up at Denver-Carrington to tell Blake that he is his son. It was not a successful reunion. Blake threw him out.

Fallon and Adam were immediately attracted to each other, not knowing that they were sister and brother.

BELOW Adam took his rightful place as the eldest Carrington child. Steven was missing in Singapore at the time this photograph was taken in 1982.

In his office at Colbyco,
Adam takes a break from his
corporate responsibilities,
1983.

Adam in his office at Denver-
Carrington, 1983. Although
he is a hard worker, it is
difficult at times to determine
whether his best interests lie
with Denver-Carrington or
with Colbyco.

When Steven returned from Singapore in 1983, Adam hoped
to establish a loving fraternal alliance. When Steven began
working at Colbyco, Adam tried to help him and was rebuffed.
Adam then deliberately let Steven fall into a trap of Alexis', a
trap designed to sabotage any possible reconciliation between
Steven and his father. Alexis' plan worked and Steven
blamed Adam.

When Jeff returned to Colbyco in 1982, Adam was doubly
jealous—jealous of the respect Alexis had for Jeff and jealous
that Kirby loved him. Adam had Jeff's office painted with a special blend that contained deadly toxins. When Alexis found out,
Adam told her that the fumes would only addle Jeff's brain
enough to make him sign papers leading the way for her take-

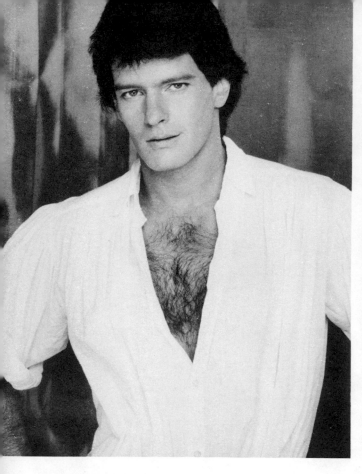 

over of Denver-Carrington. A greedy Alexis nervously went along with the plot, but when Jeff nearly died, Alexis was horrified that Adam was capable of murder and outraged when Adam made it look like *she* was the perpetrator.

Alexis bounced him out of Colbyco fast enough, but when it came to revealing the truth—that Adam had pulled the strings—her maternal love forced her to call off the merger in order to protect him. Blake believed Alexis had poisoned Jeff, but Alexis, knowing that exposing Adam would surely mean a prison term for him, said nothing. Blake hired Adam for Denver-Carrington.

Not totally without lasting emotional commitment, Adam did maintain a tremendous love for Kirby. When she was hospitalized with hyperflexia, Adam stood vigil nearly round the clock. When Kirby was near death, Adam prayed for her in the hospital chapel. Repentant, he confessed to Blake that it was he who had tried to murder Jeff. When Kirby lost their child, Adam believed that it was God's way of punishing him. Adam tried to heal Kirby's devastation with his love. When Kirby lost Jeff, Adam begged her to marry him and start life over as a Carrington.

His love eventually made Kirby at least care for him, but it is Adam's painful fate that he is consumed by love for a woman who is not in love with him. He hopes to change that, however, by marrying her.

ABOVE LEFT Adam, who grew up without a father figure, wants very much to be a father himself one day.

ABOVE RIGHT Adam and Kirby, 1984. He has been in love with her since the first time he saw her and has pleaded with her to marry him, against Alexis' wishes.

50

A brilliant lawyer, but deeply troubled young man, the broodingly handsome Adam has at last established his birthright. One can only hope that he will learn not to abuse it, and share his good fortune and love with his new family and the world.

FALLON CARRINGTON COLBY

Young Fallon Carrington was the quintessential debu-
tante—beautiful, rebellious, and bored. Her indolent
youth was misspent on the nude beaches of the Côte
d'Azur and in the steamy night spots of the jet set. The outspo-
ken and self-possessed daughter of oil baron Blake Carrington,
she is a member of America's most elite group: those for whom
everything in life has been easy. Until her twenties, she got
everything she ever wanted; she was to the manor born. Her
notion of hardship was the sight of an American Express office
closed till Monday.

Fallon was born in 1956 in Denver and grew up believing
she was the eldest Carrington child. Always Daddy's little girl,
Fallon was a clever child with a wicked sense of humor. She
was accustomed to the freedom and security only enormous
wealth can buy. Cosseted and spoiled as a child with frocks of
the finest fabric, a Shetland pony, and a forty-eight-room mansion for a playhouse, Fallon, like many an heiress before her,
became restless with her life of luxury. And, like many an heiress before her, relief from the tedium wore pants. Soccer play-
ers, race car drivers, and international playboys of every de-
scription learned that she could be as soft and sensual as
ermine, or as bright and crisp as a thousand-dollar bill.

Deeply scarred by her mother's abrupt departure when she
was nine, she had trouble sleeping for six months. When she
sought comfort, she remembers, she met her brother Steven in
the middle of the night. They'd hold hands like Hansel and
Gretel, never knowing where their mother had gone or why.

Fallon returned from Europe in 1980 for the marriage of her
father to Krystle Jennings. Shocked to learn that her father was
in financial difficulty, she hesitated not a moment when Cecil
Colby proposed to bail Blake out if she'd marry his nephew
Jeff. Although Fallon was not in love with Jeff, who had been

53

Fallon's rebellious nature was well illustrated by her skinny-dipping in the middle of Krystle's first formal dinner party at the mansion in 1980.

Though she often appears an ingenue, Fallon inherited her mother's deep-seated lust.

in love with her since they were small children, she agreed to the deal and married Jeff in Las Vegas. It was to be her and Colby's secret. Where her father was concerned, Fallon would do anything to help him.

She was miserable in the marriage from the start. Her unhappiness made her contemptuous of everything: she treated her $80,000 Clenet like a pickup, picked up lovers like dry cleaning, and brushed off her husband like lint on the hem of a Givenchy gown.

The *adult* Fallon is headstrong, high-spirited, and incredibly appealing. Her aristocratic carriage and long neck give credence to the avant-garde clothing she favors. Generous of spirit and playful, she means to strip away reserve and replace it with spontaneity. She makes no apologies. She is determined to make her own choices and her own mistakes, and she readily admits that she does both. Fallon, at long last, has become a woman and a lady.

Educated at the exclusive Miss Porter's School in Farmington, Connecticut (founded 1843), and in Europe, Fallon plays the piano, speaks fluent French and Italian, and is an outstanding equestrian and tennis player—accomplishments long associated with her station in life. She quickly drops anything she can't excel at, though when she puts her mind to it, she can succeed at almost anything.

Named after her paternal grandmother, Fallon reflects characteristics of both her parents. Like her father, whom she idolizes, she is not a person to casually cross. She has his quick temper and sharp tongue. Like her mother, she comes alive when challenged and delights in shocking people. Her antics in the past have included smoking pot and skinny-dipping in the middle of a black-tie dinner party.

When Blake found out about her affair with family chauffeur Michael, the driver was summarily threatened and later dismissed. The daughter was curtly upbraided and likened to her mother, Alexis. The comparison was not intended as flattery.

In an effort to please her father and her husband, in 1981 Fallon tried to involve herself in the Denver Junior Oil League, but she found her contemporaries too staid and predictable. With time on her hands, Fallon sought refuge in the bed of psychiatrist Nick Toscanni, whom she believed was the only man she could ever love.

Fallon discovered that she and Jeff were going to have a child. She decided on an abortion but ultimately was unable to go through with it. While driving with her mother in 1981, Fallon had an automobile accident which caused the premature delivery of her baby. As her son, little Blake, fought for his life,

The former Carrington family chauffeur, Michael. Although he kept an eye on the family and dutifully reported to Blake on their doings, his ongoing affair with Fallon after she married Jeff forced Blake to fire him.

Fallon was overtaken by a penetrating wave of maternal love she didn't know she was capable of.

In an effort to revitalize her life, Fallon broke off with Nick and tried to make her marriage work for the sake of the baby. Then tragedy occurred—little Blake was kidnapped. More fortunate than her parents had been twenty-five years before, Fallon's baby was recovered, unharmed. The kidnapper was Alfred Grimes, the father of Roger Grimes, the Carringtons' former estate manager.

With her marriage in shambles again, in 1982 Fallon took over the management of her father's hotel, La Mirada, in an effort to pull herself together. She took the old, pretentious hotel, said "In Xanadu did Kubla Khan a stately pleasure-dome decree," and vowed to remodel the hotel to match it. She found that she had an excellent head for business. Fallon thrived on her success and accomplishment as she built the new La Mirage into one of the best resort hotels in the world.

Still unhappy in her marriage, Fallon obtained a divorce from Jeff in Haiti in 1982. La Mirage continued to grow, becoming a mecca for youthful, rich, and healthy professionals. The resort's success brought her a confidence and calm assurance money never could.

In 1983, Fallon fell in love with handsome Brazilian millionaire Peter de Vilbis. When he asked her to marry him (or, rather, told the press they were engaged), the proposition sounded attractive for the first time in her life. Her father advised caution, but Fallon learned the hard way that De Vilbis was a con man and a drug addict. Basically a coward, De Vilbis could not face up to his crimes and ultimately he ran out on her. The revelation sent Fallon dashing blindly into the parking lot of La Mirage, where she was hit by a drunk driver. She was rushed to Denver Memorial, where she remained unconscious for thirty-six hours. She awoke to discover she was psychologically paralyzed from the waist down.

While Fallon was recuperating at the mansion, Jeff's kindness and love, for the first time, made a deep impression on her. One day, when she was resting outside, little Blake wandered dangerously close to the pool. Her maternal love and protectiveness freed her from her paralysis and she leaped up to save him.

Fallon in her favorite climbing tree, 1981. "I used to sit up here when I was a kid, surveying my happy world."

Unlike her father and
brothers, Fallon is rendered
vulnerable by liquor, rather
than violent.

Fallon poses with her
mother, Alexis, and brother,
Steven, 1981.

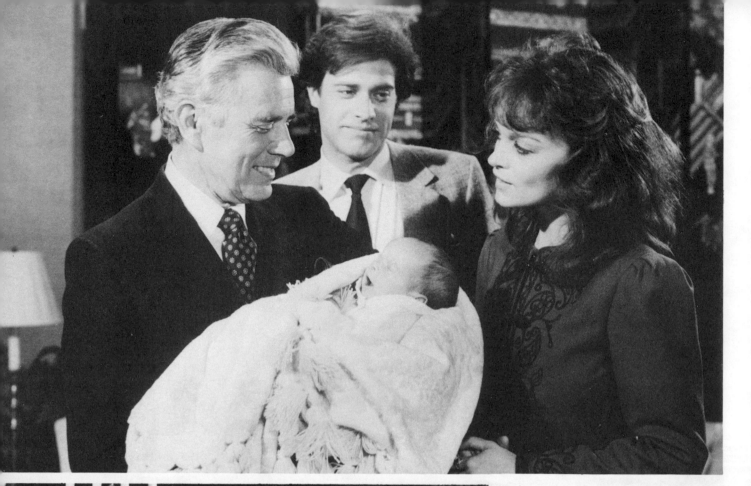

ABOVE The homecoming of little Blake Carrington Colby, in the foyer of the mansion, 1982. Born prematurely, the baby had to fight hard for his life, earning his place as the first heir to the Carrington fortune.

LEFT Jeff looks on helplessly as Fallon agonizes over the kidnapping of little Blake, 1982.

The family celebrated with a dinner which included some of her favorite palate-pleasers: roast beef, asparagus, new potatoes with sour cream and caviar, chocolate mousse, and Kristal champagne.

In 1984, Fallon and Jeff fell in love with each other, each feeling a new, and deeper, bond. They became engaged to be married, and looked forward, happily, to their future together. On the night of their wedding, however, Fallon was involved in a horrible car accident. At this writing, her life hangs in the balance.

After years of resentment toward Krystle, in 1983 Fallon realized how dear her stepmother was to her. They have been close friends ever since. (The Rolls-Royce Corniche convertible belongs to Krystle.)

ABOVE Fallon met supposed millionaire Peter de Vilbis at Hollywood Park racetrack in Los Angeles in 1983 and fell deeply in love with him, not realizing that he was a drug addict and a professional con man.

LEFT Fallon moments after being hit by a drunk driver in the parking lot of La Mirage. She was unconscious for thirty-six hours and suffered temporary paralysis. The accident occurred after Fallon learned that her fiancé, Peter, was a fraud and had run out on her.

"I fought my own battles ever since I was nine years old! I never had a mom to confide in." Though Alexis may not have been there for Fallon all those years, she did bequeath to her daughter her genes for great beauty.

JEFFREY COLBY

t is a paradox of the rite of passage that what youth disregards as stodgy and conformist, maturity regards as admirable stability. Jeff Colby, nephew and heir to the Colby fortune, has experienced this paradox from the receiving end only: Jeffrey Broderick Colby was *born* responsible. Gentle, polite, and softly handsome, he is everything one could want in a son and everything one could wish for in a husband. Jeff is a beacon of normality in the stormy Carrington sea of changeable relationships.

Orphaned as a young boy and raised "next door" to the Carringtons on Nine Oaks, the estate of his late uncle Cecil, Jeff is an acorn who did not fall far from the tree. Staunchly principled and hardworking, he is a product of the Protestant work ethic and a Princeton education.

His preferred childhood idyll was the Carrington estate, where he was a well-behaved and agreeable playmate to Fallon and Steven. It was there that he fell in love with Fallon, though she toyed with his affections as flippantly as Estella did with Pip's in *Great Expectations*. First love kindled a flame within him that grew brighter with the passing years. His lifelong dream was to marry Fallon.

In a Las Vegas wedding chapel in 1980 that dream was fulfilled, but the honeymoon was over before it began. Fallon did not love him. She married him only as a business concession conditioned on Cecil's releasing her father from his current business bind.

Life was rocky for the newlyweds. Where he was quiet, she was flamboyant; where he was tolerant, she was petulant. He was the grateful, appreciative husband, gentle and attentive. She was the impetuous, irreverent free spirit who was bitterly resentful of their marriage.

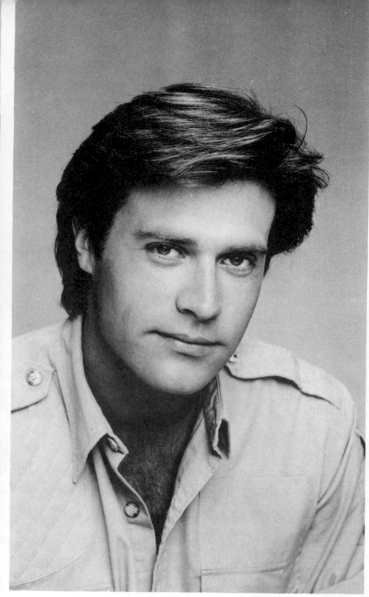

Jeff had been in love with
Fallon all his life. To marry
her, he thought, would fulfill
all his dreams.

An informal portrait.

An executive at Colbyco Oil, Jeff resigned in 1981 to protest
his uncle's questionable business practices against his father-
in-law. Blake, impressed by Jeff's principles, offered him a position with Denver-Carrington. Jeff happily accepted.

Unexpectedly finding herself pregnant, Fallon told Jeff she
was going to have an abortion. Unable to carry it through at the
last minute, she returned to the mansion for what could laugh-
ingly be called her confinement. Distinguished by his old-fash-
ioned sense of duty, Jeff decorously stood by the flighty Fallon,
until he witnessed his pregnant wife kissing Nick Toscanni.
The night his son was born prematurely, Jeff was in bed with
Claudia Blaisdel. The affair started and ended that night.

Jeff suggested the name of Blake Carrington Colby and saw
to it that their son was christened that name by the Reverend

In 1981, Fallon told Jeff why
she married him.

Mr. Carlson, the same minister who had christened both him
and Fallon.

It is hard to say whether the sturdy young Colby was more
devastated by the discovery of his wife's motives for marriage or
by the kidnapping of their infant son. The baby was recovered;
the marriage could not be. Jeff, as an orphaned child, desperately longed for a stable, loving environment for his son, and it
was tragically apparent that he and Fallon together could not
provide it. They separated, but Jeff stayed on in the mansion to
be near his son.

Jeff's uncle, Cecil Colby, died unexpectedly after marrying
Alexis Carrington. Jeff inherited half of Colbyco Oil. Feeling responsibility to his considerable fortune and mistrustful of the
devious Alexis, Jeff resumed working at Colbyco. It was a

Jeff and little Blake at Jeff's father's grave, 1982. "He hasn't been with us very long, Dad, but I love him. So very much. And I'm going to give him everything I can. Not in privileges of wealth. But, rather, in a father's caring for his son. Things like being with him when he's sick and needs me to hold his hand, tell him everything's going to be all right. Things like playing ball with him when he wants to play . . . studying with him when he needs help with his schoolwork. Simple things, Dad. Human, priceless things. The kind of things we never had a chance to share together. I love you, Dad. And my son will love you through me, always."

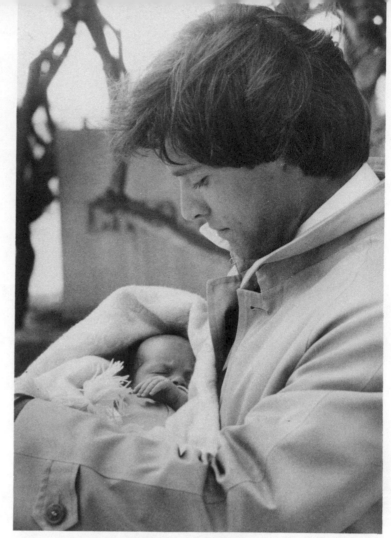

Blake and Alexis run into each other at Denver Memorial, 1983, when Jeff was hospitalized for toxic poisoning. Jeff is like a son to both of them and, like the three Carrington children, whenever something's wrong with him, Blake and Alexis are temporarily bonded with concern.

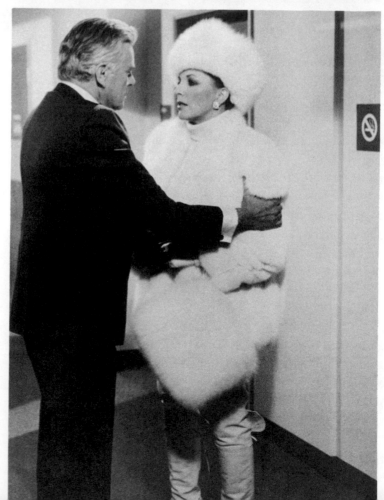

move he thought was necessary to save the family corporation from what he foresaw as destructive guidance. He accepted, as a gesture of good will, Alexis' offer to redecorate his office before his return to the company.

Unbeknown to Jeff, the fresh paint emitted lethal fumes, courtesy of Alexis' jealous son Adam Carrington. The inhalation of poisoned gases left Jeff physically and mentally debilitated. Adam's plot to eliminate the competition came perilously close to succeeding.

While in the hospital recovering from an all-too-close brush with death, Jeff was dealt another blow: Fallon had divorced him in Haiti. Nonetheless, Jeff returned to the Carrington mansion for his recovery.

In an unwitting effort to heal his wounds, in 1983 Jeff married Kirby Anders, the graceful daughter of the Carrington's majordomo, Joseph. Jeff was quick to realize that he married her

BELOW LEFT Jeff is intelligent, evenhanded, and overly earnest. He has proved to be an excellent, if not popular businessman. Here Adam visits Jeff in his Colbyco office in 1983, when his judgment was being questioned as he was being poisoned by the toxic paint on the walls of his office.

BELOW RIGHT Jeff and Fallon together in an unplanned night of loving reconciliation, in Billings, Montana, 1983. They flew up together following a lead on Adam's possible involvement in Jeff's poisoning, but they mutually agreed that the night should best be forgotten, in light of Jeff's marriage to Kirby.

ABOVE Jeff and Kirby were married in 1983. They divorced in 1984.

RIGHT Fallon has called Jeff a gentle lover, a quality she eventually came to appreciate.

not out of love, but to salve the wounds he bore from the loss of Fallon. After he learned that Kirby's unborn child was not his but Adam's, their marriage fell apart.

Not able to resolve his ethical differences with Alexis, Jeff forced her to trade her Denver-Carrington stock for his Colbyco stock, and Blake happily welcomed him back to Denver-Carrington.

Prospects for happiness seem to be on the rise for Jeff Colby. Brought together in mutual love this time, Fallon and Jeff have rekindled their relationship. The older and wiser Fallon finally appreciates the stability that she dismissed as stodgy in her youth. The conventional, gentlemanly Jeff has gained the long-overdue validation for being the earnest and honorable man he always was.

70

Jeff has a wry sense of
humor. He claims the Colby
motto is, "Never put off
beyond tomorrow what you
can do tomorrow."

STEVEN CARRINGTON

Steven Daniel Carrington was born on June 7, 1958, under the sign of Gemini, the Twins. Scion of the Carrington oil fortune, Steven is sometimes stoic, other times cheerful and outgoing. Frequently his speech is slow and measured; just as often it is heatedly argumentative. He has been characterized by gentlemanly reserve; he has at other times appeared a violent drunk. A study in contradictions, he might at one moment be absorbed in his books, the next moment planning a career as a race car driver. He is currently happily married to Claudia Blaisdel; he has been a practicing homosexual.

> In 1640, Ben Jonson wrote: "Greatness of name in the father oft-times overwhelms the son; they stand too near one another. The shadow kills the growth . . ."

Steven was to bear the Carrington name like a cross. He felt the tremendous pressure of a son born to a highly successful father and doubted if he could ever live up to Blake's expectations. He was his mother's favorite, and Blake accused Alexis of coddling him too much. Steven also unknowingly bore the additional burden of replacing the son whom his parents had lost in 1957.

At age five, Steven nearly died of pneumonia. The vigil of his parents and their extra ministrations saved his life. But Steven viewed it as a command not to die, under penalty of death.

He still remembers the tears he shed when his mother abandoned the family three days before his seventh birthday. He felt the pain of rejection by his mother and, at the same time, blamed his father for driving her away. His loving relationship with his sister Fallon was one of the few joys in his growing-up years. It was a childhood fraught with Freudian implications.

ABOVE LEFT Working at the drilling site of Matthew Blaisdel and Walter Lankershim's oil rig, 1980.

ABOVE RIGHT Unmercifully taunted about his homosexuality by his coworkers, Steven proved to be as good with his fists as he was on the job.

RIGHT Steven and Sammy Jo Dean shortly before they eloped in 1981. Sammy Jo inspired Steven's brief career as a race car driver. (The estate tennis court can be seen in the background.)

Steven was never as outgoing as the bright Fallon. He felt it difficult to match her vivacity, and when it came to people, he preferred to retreat to his books. He found Emily Dickinson:

How dreary—to be—Somebody!
How public—like a Frog—
To tell one's name—the livelong June—
To an admiring Bog!

Steven was sent away to Choate, the prep school in Wallingford, Connecticut. From there he went on to Princeton, where he resided in Stafford Little Hall, waiting futilely for his father to visit him on parents' weekend. At graduation, his father arrived.

A sensitive, artistic young man, unsure of what to do with his life, Steven was certain only that he could never follow in his father's footsteps. Upon graduation in 1979, Steven moved to New York. Despite his background (which Fallon described as "a world where culls and cripples and homosexuals are taken out behind the barn and slaughtered before they can breed"), Steven allowed himself to fall in love with another man. Steven and his lover, Ted Dinard, lived together in a Greenwich Village walk-up apartment.

In the cultural center of the country, Steven and Ted Dinard shared art, music, and the theater. A subscriber to the Metropolitan Opera season, Steven still recalls the thrilling high "C" of "Che gelida manina" when Luciano Pavarotti triumphed as Rodolfo in Puccini's *La Bohème*.

When Steven arrived back in Denver for his father's wedding to Krystle Jennings, his relationship with Ted was over, but the storm that had been brewing for years between father and son erupted with fury. Resentful of his father's demands, that he "straighten out his life and work at Denver-Carrington," Steven took a job on competitor Matthew Blaisdel's oil-drilling site.

Ted wanted to renew his relationship with Steven, but Steven wanted first to find himself. Fallon urged Steven to remain in Denver and even flew to San Francisco to beg Ted to stay out of Steven's life. To complicate things further, Steven began an affair with his boss's wife, Claudia Blaisdel. She had recently been released from a sanatorium, but Steven found her far from mad. She was warm, compassionate, bright, and shared his passion for literature. It was a time of personal exploration for both of them.

Plagued by accusations of sabotaging the rig and taunted by his coworkers about his homosexuality, Steven resigned from his job. Resolute to start life anew, in 1981, he rented his own

Steven and Sammy Jo were married in Reno in 1981.

apartment, enrolled in night-school business courses, and took a job at Denver-Carrington. In an attempt to patch things up with his father, he committed himself to his new life. What seemed like the beginning of a conditional amnesty was merely the lull before battle.

Ted Dinard came to Denver to make his last play for Steven, but they mutually agreed the affair was over for good. As they were saying their final good-byes at the mansion, Blake's untimely arrival interrupted their embrace. Blake, in a fit of temper, pushed Dinard away from his son. Ted fell, hit his head, and died. Blake was charged with manslaughter, convicted, and sentenced to two years' probation.

Ted's death, which further estranged father and son, seemed to destroy any hope of reconciliation. Blake, on the brink of losing Denver-Carrington in the wake of his conviction, couldn't deal with Steven. Steven, submerged in grief and anguish, couldn't deal with Blake. Father and son began drinking heavily.

76

ABOVE Blake and Alexis in Indonesia, 1982, where they went to search for Steven after the oil rig he was working on exploded.

RIGHT Sammy Jo, 1982. She returned to the mansion with a new baby and a new name, Samantha Dean.

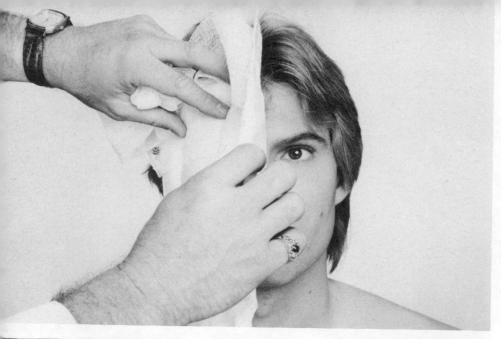

Steven as his bandages were removed in Singapore.

It is an emotional homecoming for Steven at the Carrington Mansion after his hospitalization in Singapore, 1983. Blake had called ahead to warn the family that Steven looked very different; the plastic surgeon had no model to go by when he reconstructed Steven's face after the explosion. But the family didn't care. Steven was home!

An adoring Fallon is overcome by seeing her brother again, new face or not.

Steven sees his son, Steven Daniel Carrington, Jr., for the first time.

Steven meets the older brother he never knew he had.

Steven and Sammy Jo, a.k.a. Samantha, dining in Greenwich Village, 1983. Steven flew to New York to try to save their marriage for the sake of their son, but Samantha was not willing to change her life-style.

A drunken Steven went to the mansion to attempt a détente. Steven fled the confrontation with his father, stumbled, and hit his head on the pool diving board. He was unconscious in the pool when Nick Toscanni rescued him. Steven was rushed to the hospital with possible brain damage.

Having returned to the mansion for his recovery, Steven met Sammy Jo Dean, Krystle's niece. Sammy Jo came West when she learned of Krystle's change of fortune. Krystle gladly welcomed her to the mansion because Krystle had so loved her sister, Iris, who had died some time ago. Sammy Jo grew up on the racing car circuit with her father after her mother's death. The young, hardened blonde was anxious to assume the Carrington wealth and so she seduced Steven.

Steven was still in love with Claudia Blaisdel but was entertained by Sammy Jo. When Claudia refused his marriage proposal, Steven was at a loss. He ran off to Reno, where he and Sammy Jo were secretly married. After their return, they made two announcements: they were married and Steven was resigning from Denver-Carrington to become a professional race car driver.

Between modeling shoots, Sammy Jo reads about the custody suit in the *Enquirer* and decides to testify against Steven, hoping Blake will pay her to do so. Blake refused to have anything to do with her, but she flew to Denver anyway.

In 1983, Steven resumed his love relationship with Claudia Blaisdel, following her release from the sanatorium.

The Carrington family was mortified, and the couple's happiness was short-lived. Sammy Jo was piqued to learn that Steven had no money of his own and that she couldn't spend Blake's. Alexis, who nearly had a stroke when she learned of the marriage, offered Sammy Jo twenty-five thousand dollars to leave Steven. Cash in hand, Miss Dean left for Hollywood and Vine to "be discovered."

In 1982, on his way home after a futile trip to Los Angeles to persuade Sammy Jo to return with him, Steven picked up a drifter named Duane. Duane attempted to blackmail Steven by claiming Steven had made sexual overtures to him. Steven lost his Carrington temper, scuffled with Duane, and was arrested for assault. Blake assumed that Steven *had* made a pass at the man, and a fight severed affection between Steven and Blake again. An angry and hurt Steven left Denver to work on a drilling platform off one of the islands of Indonesia.

Later that year, an explosion demolished the offshore platform and Steven drifted in the wreckage for days. The Carringtons were told he was missing and presumed dead. Unconscious, Steven was rescued and, identity unknown, was hospitalized in Singapore. His face was horribly disfigured from the fiery holocaust. The total facial reconstruction that was necessary left him looking like a different person.

Sammy Jo (who now insisted on being called Samantha), read about Steven's presumed death in the newspapers and brought her newborn baby to the Carrington estate. It was Steven's son, Steven Daniel Carrington, Jr. She left the boy (called Danny) with Krystle and Blake, who planned to adopt him, and moved to New York to become a model.

Blake spent a fortune in search of Steven, whom everyone else had given up for dead. Time, distance, and paternal love contributed to his genuine heartache. So determined was he to find Steven, Blake even hired a psychic to help in the search. Finally, in 1983, Steven was located and Blake went to Singapore to bring him back to Denver. Steven, not so quick to trust Blake's pacifism, only returned to see his son Danny.

After a reunion with his family, which now included his long-lost brother Adam, Steven flew to New York to attempt a reconciliation with Sammy Jo. His efforts were unsuccessful, however, and they decided to get a divorce. Steven was to retain custody of Danny.

With a new face and a new life ahead of him with his son, Steven borrowed money from Fallon to set up housekeeping in his own Denver apartment. He accepted his mother's offer of a job with Colbyco, and he quietly began to see Claudia Blaisdel again.

His tranquility was brief, however. When Chris Deegan, his divorce lawyer, came to Denver, Steven allowed him to stay at his apartment. Blake erroneously assumed they were lovers and sued for custody of Danny, fearful of the effect a gay household would have on his grandson and heir.

The custody hearing was a nightmare. The family was bitterly at odds. Steven, refusing on principle to denounce the implied homosexual relationship, was sure to lose Danny. His salvation came; Claudia thought of it. They flew to Reno and were married. Presented with their marriage certificate, the court dismissed the suit, assured of Steven's sexual preference and implied fitness as a guardian.

Steven and Claudia remained deeply in love, but their happiness was threatened by Alexis' machinations. With Claudia and Steven both working, they had hired a nurse to care for Danny during the day. The nurse reported that a strange man had been following her and Danny, and fearful of the possibility of a kidnapping, Steven, Danny, and Claudia moved into the Carrington mansion in 1984.

Their future for the moment seems bright with promise. Steven is gratified that his relationship with Blake is conciliatory, but he is cautious, remembering the words of Winston Churchill, "This is not the end. It is not even the beginning of the end. But it is, perhaps, the end of the beginning."

83

A troubled Blake with Andrew Laird at the custody hearing, 1983.

Steven and Chris Deegan on their side of the courtroom, with Alexis and Krystle looking on.

Alexis and Krystle in the ladies' room of the courthouse. Oddly enough, during the custody trial, both ladies were on the same side—Steven's, not Blake's.

At the height of the custody trial in 1983, Steven and Claudia flew to Reno and were married. The marriage won Steven custody of his son and, perhaps just as important, the woman he loves.

CLAUDIA BLAISDEL CARRINGTON

If there was an axiom like Catch-22 about psychiatrists, it might be posed as a question: Is anyone who's crazy enough to *want* to explore the reaches of the human mind, sane enough to define sanity? Claudia Blaisdel, the fragile, lovely, and now sane wife of Steven Carrington, would surely like to hear the answer.

Never certain where the division between sanity and insanity lay, Claudia has always been surprised how arbitrarily it is assigned. Considering the circumstances of her life, it has struck her as ironic that what was considered totally normal in one person is flatly unacceptable in another.

Though she's had her mental ups and downs, been suicidal, homicidal, institutionalized, and otherwise labeled "out to lunch," she is not ashamed of it. Her bond with Steven, and what initially drew them together, was the shared conviction that everything in life must be questioned, paths explored internally and externally, and only then can one choose from the alternatives.

Her life as a Carrington is pleasant enough, but in the back of her mind she worries that the instabilities of her past will continue to haunt her. At times she believes she is trying to build a new castle on a house of cards.

At sixteen, Claudia Barrows met Matthew Blaisdel, a nineteen-year-old cowboy. He drove to school from a ranch in a pickup truck, and bore the inviting scent of fresh-cut alfalfa. Their splendor in the grass resulted in pregnancy. Claudia, terrified and ashamed, ran away and hid. Finally, one night, she called Matthew and broke the news. Two days later they were married. Their daughter Lindsay was born in 1968.

Warm, kind, gentle, and intelligent, Claudia has had more than her share of emotional traumas in recent years.

Matthew Blaisdel, Claudia's first love and husband. He worked at Denver-Carrington for many years but resigned in 1980 to strike out on his own as a wildcatter.

Unremarkable years passed by for Claudia as Matthew first graduated from the Colorado School of Mines, then made a career for himself in the oil fields of Denver-Carrington. But suddenly in 1978, Claudia experienced a complete mental breakdown that sent her, in her own words, "running down the street shrieking about devil worshippers and smashing car windows with a croquet mallet." Her husband and daughter became frozen onlookers as three policemen dragged her off in a straitjacket, thrashing and frothing at the mouth.

She was institutionalized for a year and a half. Lindsay was placed in the care of Mother Blaisdel, and Matthew took a high-paying overseas assignment in the Middle East to meet the cost of her treatment.

Released as an outpatient in 1980, she was scared to return to her husband and child. She took a job as a waitress for a month, but her family convinced her to come home. She reestablished her good relations with Lindsay, but her relationship with Matthew continued to be strained. He had resigned from Denver-Carrington and struck out on his own as a wildcatter with Walter Lankershim, and the new venture, fraught with problems, kept Matthew at the drilling site for endless hours.

Claudia with daughter Lindsay and Matthew, shortly after her release from High Meadow Sanatorium in 1980. Family relations were strained to the breaking point by Claudia's psychological instability.

ABOVE Walter Lankershim and Matthew Blaisdel trying their skill and luck as wildcatters, as Blake Carrington had some twenty-five years before.

LEFT Steven trying to comfort Claudia in Denver Memorial Hospital, 1981. After testifying at the Dinard trial that she was having an affair with Steven, she suffered a car accident on the way home.

ABOVE Claudia consulting with lawyer Andrew Laird about getting Lindsay back from Matthew in South America. Sadly, Andrew warned her against seeking custody, since her testimony at the Dinard trial would have made the courts label her an unfit mother.

RIGHT Dr. Nick Toscanni, a psychiatrist and former practicing surgeon, picked up the scalpel again in 1982 to remove the bullet from Claudia's brain. It saved her life, and as a psychiatrist, he tried to save her sanity.

Lonely, eager to be productive, Claudia worked part-time in a bookstore. But it did not fill the void caused by Matthew's distracted interest.

In 1981, Claudia had an affair and fell in love with the most unlikely man in all of Denver—Steven Carrington. The affair tortured Claudia; she still loved her distant husband, Matthew, and felt deep responsibilities toward her daughter, but Steven gave her the love and patient understanding she needed so desperately.

Nineteen eighty-one turned out to be a hellish year for her. At the highly publicized manslaughter trial of Blake Carrington, Steven's homosexuality was unmercifully dragged into court. Against Steven's wishes, Claudia was called to testify, and in an effort to prove that Steven and Ted Dinard were not lovers at the time of the murder, Claudia confessed their affair. Matthew, after hearing his wife's testimony, lunged at Blake, angry that Blake caused him this public humiliation. Matthew was restrained and taken away by bailiffs. Hysterical, Claudia had a serious automobile accident on the way home. Hospitalized, she learned when she came to that Matthew had left town with Lindsay. They were on their way to South America.

Despondent over her loss and feeling totally helpless, Claudia attempted suicide with an overdose of sleeping pills. Blake Carrington and psychiatrist Nick Toscanni discovered the overdose in time to save her life. Blake insisted that she move into his mansion for rest and recuperation (and to keep an eye on her). Claudia did, but beneath the surface festered the strain of her loss.

Claudia also accepted Blake's offer of a job at Denver-Carrington. She was so obsessed about getting information on the whereabouts of her husband and daughter, she became an industrial spy for Cecil Colby. In return, he had promised to locate Matthew and Lindsay. So desperate was she that one night she even seduced Jeff Colby and, while he was asleep, stole the keys to his office to finish a job for Colby. Jeff caught her. Plagued by guilt, Claudia confessed to Blake and tried to resign from Denver-Carrington. Blake forgave her and persuaded her to remain.

Claudia soon discovered that Cecil Colby had been stringing her along, knowing that Matthew and Lindsay were presumed dead in a Peruvian jungle. She also learned for sure that Matthew, while Claudia had been in the sanatorium, had had an affair with the then Krystle Jennings before he left for the Middle East. Crazed with grief and anger, Claudia got a gun and was on her way to kill Colby when Krystle tried to stop her. They struggled, and the gun went off, sending a bullet into Claudia's brain.

ABOVE Attending Steven's
memorial service, 1982.

RIGHT Claudia the day she
was released from Hackley-
Morris Sanatorium in 1983.

Nick Toscanni (formerly a brain surgeon before becoming a psychiatrist) removed the bullet and Claudia narrowly missed permanent damage. During her recovery, Claudia refused to tell the police that the incident was an accident, choosing to punish Krystle for her affair by allowing the police to believe that Krystle tried to murder her. Claudia finally broke down and told the truth. She and Krystle, who under other circumstances would have been friends, made an uneasy truce which in later years blossomed into genuine friendship. Claudia moved into the Carrington mansion, where she sadly turned Steven down when he proposed spending their lives together.

In 1982, Claudia truly lapsed into a fantasy world. She refused to believe that her daughter was dead and when Fallon and Jeff Colby's infant son, little Blake, was kidnapped and Claudia disappeared, they chased her, assuming she was the kidnapper. When they found her, Claudia dashed to the rooftop of a building carrying what looked like the baby. It wasn't. The tiny body that slipped from Claudia's fingers and plummeted

Claudia confronts Sammy Jo about her false testimony at the custody trial, 1983.

down to the ground was a doll. But poor Claudia did not know the difference. She was committed to the Hackley-Morris Sanatorium.

A year later, Claudia was released and she started working as a banquet manager for Fallon at La Mirage. When Steven was divorcing Sammy Jo in 1983, they resumed their relationship. During the custody hearing that Blake initiated against Steven because of his alleged homosexual life-style, Claudia, acting quickly so Steven would not have to endure the pain that she had undergone in losing a child, suggested that they prove Steven's sexuality and fitness as a parent by getting married. They flew to Reno, married, and the custody case was dismissed.

In 1984, Claudia was haunted by the arrival of flowers and messages so personal that they appeared to have come from Matthew. Then she received a phone call—it *was* Matthew's voice. Near hysteria, Claudia flew to Peru to find out once and for all if Matthew, and possibly her daughter, *could* be alive. Steven followed her there in loving support, ready to help her,

Claudia and Steven being married in a wedding chapel, Reno, 1983, as Danny looks on.

whatever the news. Claudia was shown the wreckage of the Jeep they had been in and she was told that the bodies were never recovered.

Exhausted, frightened still, the Steven Carringtons returned to Denver and there the mystery was solved. A private detective had obtained one of Matthew's taped letters from his mother (who blamed Claudia for the deaths of her son and granddaughter). Now knowing for sure that Matthew was dead, Claudia could resume her life.

If nothing else, these difficult years have given this complex survivor the confidence of her sanity, the splendor of love with Steven and their son, Danny, and the affirmation of her dear friends and in-laws, Blake and Krystle Carrington. Claudia continues to grow stronger, taking life one day at a time.

Claudia with her mother-in-law, Mrs. Blaisdel, 1984, not knowing she was behind the messages from Matthew.

Claudia, 1984, during the time she was being haunted by flowers, messages, a photograph, and a phone call supposedly from her dead ex-husband, Matthew.

KIRBY ANDERS COLBY

A well-known adage observes that there are two families in this world, the "haves" and the "have-nots." Most children grow up well aware of the berth in which they have secured passage for this voyage. The evidence is painfully obvious. This helps prepare them for their adult life, when the difference will be flung in their faces.

The dichotomy of Kirby Alicia Anders is curious in this regard: she was under the distinct impression that she belonged to the "haves." The case was prima facie: she lived in a forty-eight-room mansion all her life; luxurious automobiles overflowed the garages; sideboards were arched with silver service; sumptuous food abounded; imposing paintings adorned the silk-covered walls. Opulence surrounded her; the gravy train stopped at her door.

When she was eleven, the jury came in. They told her flatly and irrefutably that she belonged to the "have-nots." Though little Kirby was raised in the lap of luxury, someone just stood up, and she was dumped unceremoniously on a very bare floor.

Kirby is the daughter of the Carrington family majordomo, Joseph Anders. Originally retained by Alexis, Joseph headed the household staff for nearly as long as the Carringtons have occupied the mansion. Kirby had two siblings and believed, as her father told her, that her mother died when she was three.

While growing up, Kirby assumed she was a branch of the Carrington family tree, not the scrubwood beneath it. With free run of the house and grounds, and observing her father in a managerial position, she thought she was equal to Fallon and Steven. When she discovered she was a second-class citizen, it hurt her deeply. She was a part of the Carrington empire, but not *of* the Carringtons.

Kirby returned from Europe in 1982, where she studied at the Sorbonne.

Joseph Anders, Kirby's father, the Carrington majordomo, and Blake's loyal friend.

Joseph sent Kirby to the Continent to study. By the time she enrolled in the Sorbonne, the institute of theology, science, and literature founded in 1252, Kirby spoke French like a native and knew Paris like the back of her hand. Her education also included the arts; she demonstrated proficiency in both classical piano and ballet.

While abroad, Kirby became romantically involved with Jean-Paul Cadot. Kirby fell hard for this wealthy Frenchman from an old-line family, but it turned out he was just a well-heeled playboy. Before she realized he was married, Kirby enthusiastically told her father that they were engaged. After she realized he was married, she accompanied him to jet-set parties in Monte Carlo, Deauville, and Nice.

When the affair ended, Kirby took a job as a baby's nanny on board a yacht in the Mediterranean. It was not the life of her dreams and, at twenty-one, Kirby was not about to throw her dreams overboard. She returned to Denver before Christmas 1982.

Kirby is greeted by her father, Joseph, at her homecoming to the Carrington estate.

Fallon was delighted at Kirby's return and hired her as nanny for little Blake. Kirby's intelligence and innate poise helped her fit in with the Carrington household.

From the moment she arrived, Adam had eyes for this poignant, fragile beauty. The fun in her eyes was mixed with a good dose of mischief. Kirby was not interested in Adam's advances; since childhood, she had had a crush on Jeff. Now that Jeff's long love of Fallon was played out and they were getting a divorce, Kirby believed she had a chance. Kirby and Jeff were married in Reno in 1983. The downstairs girl was at last the upstairs bride.

The Carringtons graciously accepted Kirby as a member of their family. Alexis Colby did not.

Kirby discovered and was elated that she was pregnant. But then she was thrown into despair, realizing that having been raped by Adam three months before, it was *his* baby, not Jeff's, that she was carrying.

When her father committed suicide, Blake broke the news to

Kirby. She was devastated and felt more alone than ever before.

The relationship between Kirby and her husband never really had a chance, since Jeff still loved Fallon. Things between them disintegrated, but they kept their problems to themselves. When they decided to divorce, they waited to tell the family until after Blake and Krystle returned from their honeymoon.

Plagued by toxemia during pregnancy, Kirby's hands began to swell. When her wedding ring had to be cut off her finger because it was blocking the flow of blood, it symbolized the end of her relationship with Jeff. With her very life in danger, Kirby was taken to the hospital. Under the pending threat that the baby would die, and possibly Kirby as well, Adam and the Carringtons stood by her in the hospital. When the baby died, Adam realized how deep his love for Kirby was. He asked her to marry him.

While recovering from her miscarriage at the Carrington mansion, Kirby agreed to marry Adam when her divorce from Jeff was final.

Alexis, however, was determined this marriage would not happen. Convinced that Kirby was not the "right" girl for her eldest son, Alexis invited Kirby to her penthouse to discuss it.

Alexis had it all mapped out: if Kirby would take a job in Colbyco's Paris office, she would get a $25,000 bonus and a beautiful apartment, and all her expenses would be covered. When Kirby scoffed at the offer, Alexis brought out the heavy artillery. She presented Kirby with a collection of articles that she'd obtained from the files of the Denver *Chronicle*. The articles, now fifteen years old, told of a woman who murdered her lover and was convicted and imprisoned at a facility for the criminally insane. The woman was Kirby's mother.

Kirby reeled. She thought the death of her father had left her an orphan; she had always believed her mother was dead.

Kirby left immediately for the North Dakota prison that held her mother. When she arrived, she learned her mother had been released three weeks earlier. Investigating further, she discovered her mother had committed suicide. At the gravesite marked Anders, Kirby wept.

Returning home, Kirby steeled her resolve to be Mrs. Adam Carrington. Hurt deeply by Alexis, Kirby also fortified herself with the thought of her revenge. She bought a pistol and took lessons in how to use it. Her fierce determination made her a quick study; she was more than just comfortable with a gun, she was armed and deadly. Alexis has narrowly escaped being murdered by Kirby once.

But perhaps Alexis has finally met her match in the little girl who is only a servant's daughter.

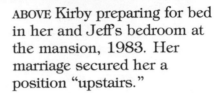

ABOVE Kirby preparing for bed in her and Jeff's bedroom at the mansion, 1983. Her marriage secured her a position "upstairs."

BELOW Kirby in pain, unable to tell her husband Jeff the truth about who the father of her unborn child is.

BELOW Joseph Anders set the fire to kill Alexis, who had threatened to tell Kirby about her real mother.

II.
THE EMPIRE

THE CARRINGTON MANSION AND ESTATE

The crowning jewel of the Carrington empire is the peerless forty-eight-room Georgian mansion the family calls home. Designed by architect Willis Polk and built in 1915, the magnificent house, situated on a wooded 645-acre estate, is unquestionably Denver's finest. In addition to the house, the grounds feature a tennis court, swimming pool, art studio, stable, coach house, and various outbuildings.

Broad lawned terraces surround the main house. A stone balustrade separates the terraces from the parterre, topiary, and rose gardens. The exquisite sixteen-acre formal gardens were designed by Bruce Porter in the classical Italian manner and took over seven years to complete.

The aroma of rose mingles with gardenia to perfume the rarefied air. It is hard to believe this heaven is on earth.

The Carrington mansion is more than just an imposing building and verdant gardens suitable for a dynasty, it is a home for a family—alternately shelter from the storm of outside events and the eye of the hurricane for family imbroglios. Reflecting the taste of its owners, Blake and Krystle Carrington, the home is both elegant and comfortable.

As one passes through the portal, the handcarved Venetian mahogany lanterns on either side catch the eye. The main foyer is carpeted with a rare oriental in shades of green that are echoed by the fresh flowers and pots of cymbidiums. The ambiance is inviting, projecting a warm welcome to family and visitor alike.

Luncheon is generally served at twelve-thirty. Family and guests may lunch in the dining room, though Krystle often prefers to have lunch poolside or in the solarium, where the profusion of plants and flowers make eating almost an alfresco experience.

After optional cocktails and canapes on the terrace or in the living room, dinner is served promptly at eight, and everyone is expected to dress. The dining room itself is dominated by the four-and-a-half-foot French antique crystal chandelier. The three-pedestal Duncan Phyfe table is beautifully laid with linen placemats and the dinner service, Wedgwood bone china in the Charnwood pattern. (Formal occasions call for the cobalt blue and gold Legacy pattern by Valhalla.) The table is surrounded by Chippendale chairs. The Baccarat crystal stemware reflects the soft glow of candlelight.

A typical dinner entrée is roast duckling (Blake's favorite), which is prepared in the expansive kitchen by Mrs. Gunnerson, Colorado's most renowned cook.

After dinner, V.S.O.P. Napoleon brandy is poured from Waterford decanters in the library, where the family gathers around the fireplace to share the events of the day. The rich colors and deep leather sofas contribute to the atmosphere of conviviality.

Krystle walking toward the right side of the mansion, where the terrace leads into the conservatory.

Blake and Krystle enjoy a casual dinner on the back terrace.

Claudia and Alexis chat by the estate pool during Claudia's stay with the Carringtons in 1981.

Breakfast is served from seven-thirty to nine daily. The menu may include shirred or scrambled eggs, omelettes, eggs Benedict; honey ham, bacon, sausage, or steak; muffins or croissants. Fresh floral arrangements are brought daily to the mansion and vary seasonally according to what is naturally in bloom.

The library is a favorite spot for after-dinner brandy. Hundreds of leather-bound first editions line the walls. An antique globe and the red, gray, and blue antique oriental rug are impressive room accessories. Of special note are the handcarved mahogany statue of a member of the Vatican's Swiss Guard, circa 1750, and a pair of Empire satinwood side tables valued at $14,000 each.

Blake meets with members of the household staff, in the library. The mansion contains many fine examples of decorative arts, including antique oriental rugs and silver, handcarved mahogany lecterns, paintings of the late 1800s, and a Ming Dynasty vase.

ABOVE Blake with his daughter in Fallon and Jeff's bedroom. The antique bed was restored and shipped from France especially for this room.

RIGHT The mansion nursery is the cheerful domain of little Blake and Danny, who are frequently visited by their doting family.

Blake reprimanding the servants in the kitchen, 1980. Because of Krystle's working-class background, the staff initially dismissed their new mistress' orders, but Krystle's inherent sense of taste and fair play soon won their love and respect.

111

DENVER-CARRINGTON

Towering over downtown Denver is the thirty-five-story headquarters of international oil giant Denver-Carrington. Beginning in 1959, with a single well, the company's astounding growth is attributed to its founder, Blake Carrington. In this, its silver anniversary year, Denver-Carrington operates hundreds of productive wells, primarily in the American Southwest, the Middle East, and Southeast Asia. Expanding interests include refineries, tankers, and reclamation, including an exclusive, pioneering oil-shale extraction process.

Though the corporation has offices around the world, Chairman of the Board and Chief Operating Officer Carrington keeps his board the exclusive province of Eastern-educated white, Anglo-Saxon Protestants.

Industry analysts have long looked to Denver-Carrington when predicting the future of the oil industry. With diversified holdings and financial interests in the hundreds of millions, Denver-Carrington qualifies as an empire. It is no accident that the New York office is just three blocks from Wall Street.

LEFT It all began here. Blake's first oil well gave birth to what is now the international conglomerate Denver-Carrington.

Founder, Chairman of the Board, and Chief Operating Officer of Denver-Carrington, Blake Carrington. When business takes him around the world, Blake always flies first class—aboard Denver-Carrington's Lear Jet Star or Cessna Citation or Falcon.

BELOW LEFT Public Relations Chief of Denver-Carrington, Krystle Carrington, in her office with her former assistant, Tracy Kendall, and Blake Carrington, 1983. Tracy was eventually dismissed for the attempted seduction of Blake.

BELOW RIGHT Tracy Kendall working on a P.R. campaign celebrating Denver-Carrington's twenty-fifth anniversary in 1984.

VIPs from all over the world are familiar faces at Denver-Carrington. Congressman Neil McVane consults with Blake about trouble on Capitol Hill, 1983.

ABOVE As with Colbyco, Denver-Carrington is fully equipped to provide refreshments to its distinguished executives and their guests.

LEFT Blake meets Krystle after spending a Saturday morning at the office. In the background is the Denver-Carrington building.

115

Cecil Colby, the longtime Chairman of the Board of Colbyco. He passed away in 1982.

BELOW Colbyco's Chief Executive Officer, Alexis Carrington Colby. She confesses she got F's in arithmetic, but the Colbyco balance sheet is testimony to her straight A's in high finance.

COLBYCO OIL

The Colbys have been in the United States for almost four hundred years. They undertook empire-building early in the War of 1812 and haven't stopped since. What started as a manufacturing concern, grew, invested, adapted, and filled a growing country's needs as they arose. With the advent of the automobile, the Colbys foresaw the demand for fossil fuel. As generation passed the business to generation, their market share increased. By the time the post-World War II family moved to their suburban utopia, Colbyco Oil was a national fixture, and when leadership of the family business was inherited by Cecil Colby, it looked as if nothing could shake Colbyco from its lead far ahead of the pack.

In the West especially, oil was the exclusive realm of Colbyco. Until, that is, upstart Denver-Carrington built itself into a threat against all odds and without outside venture capital. It used to be said that Colbyco made Denver-Carrington look like a corner filling station. Cecil Colby should have foreseen the insatiable drive of his close friend, Blake Carrington. Today the companies are rival titans.

Shortly before his death, Cecil Colby married Carrington's ex-wife, Alexis. With this celebrated wonderwoman at the helm, Colbyco abandoned its staid, old-line tradition and inaugurated a corporate stance that made the Four Horsemen of the Apocalypse look laid back.

In 1983, Colbyco came close to acquiring Denver-Carrington in a move carefully choreographed by Alexis Carrington Colby. At the eleventh hour, the near merger fell through.

Critics charge the aggressive Mrs. Colby with spending too much time countering Denver-Carrington moves and too little time forerunning. Perhaps the critics underestimate Mrs. Colby. With operations around the world, especially in Latin and South America, Colbyco's Lear Jetstream II is often in the air. It is a metaphor for the corporation—always on the move.

Fallon looking over the interior-design plans for La Mirage, 1982.

Fallon: " 'In Xanadu did Kubla Khan a stately pleasure-dome decree.' That's what I want my hotel to be."

Designer: "Like a Class-A bordello."

Fallon: "Not quite."

Fallon hired tennis pro Mark Jennings for La Mirage in 1982. Jennings was an expert not only in tennis, but also in affairs of the heart. He romanced Alexis, Fallon, and his ex-wife Krystle during his tenure there.

LA MIRAGE

When Blake Carrington gave his daughter Fallon one of his properties to manage in 1982, neither of them expected the triumphant results. Especially Fallon. Her first tour of the hotel left her with three observations: wicker furniture abounded on the porches, the guests were "barely alive," and the recreational thrills were canasta, croquet, and bowling on the green.

Hotel La Mirada, where the watchword was "sedate," was *not* what the sprightly Fallon had in mind. So she hired theatrical designer Billy Dawson to remodel it under her supervision. The caterpillar emerged from its chrysalis, a sensational resort hotel for the very youthful, very tanned, and very rich.

When she was ready to unveil the fruit of her energetic labors—La Mirage—Fallon decided on a Roaring Twenties Ball, figuring that was probably the last time the place had seen a really good party.

Guided by her inspired and vigorous direction, La Mirage has flourished. Guests swim, play tennis or golf, exercise, or just bend an elbow in the Matador Bar. The restaurant serves well-prepared and well-presented food for every palate. The friendly staff is attentive and ready to cater to a guest's smallest whim.

And proprietress Fallon, like her father, never satisfied, plans to make La Mirage even more luxurious and even more popular. The resort will undergo extensive renovations later this year.

ABOVE AND BELOW La Mirage attracts the international jet set. In 1984, the world-renowned singer and nightclub owner from Europe, Dominique Devereaux, stayed there.

RIGHT Alexis poses with Dominique. Both women are world-renowned beauties.

III.
THE CARRINGTONS AT HOME AND PLAY

The Carringtons play as hard as they work. They know that the key to maintaining their stunning good looks and robust good health lies in exercise and stress-relieving leisure-time activities. Every one of them works out daily, and has his or her own hobbies and interests that keep them mentally sharp.

One of Krystle's greatest joys in becoming a Carrington was learning to ride with the best. The estate has its own stable, trainers, and stableboys. All of the Carringtons are accomplished equestrians. On the estate they always ride English saddle; up in the mountains, western.

LEFT Blake regularly works out his stress by swimming laps in the estate pool.

BELOW LEFT Krystle enjoys swimming as well.

BELOW RIGHT Adam works out daily and is an avid swimmer, too. It shows.

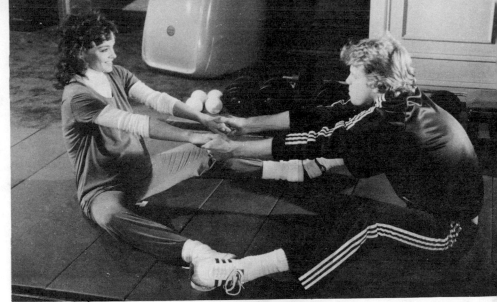

Steven teaching pregnant Fallon the "rowboat" in the mansion exercise room, 1982. Steven regularly works out with weights; Adam, Jeff, and Krystle also exercise here daily.

With her mother looking on, Fallon shoots skeet on the Carrington estate. Fallon is good, but Alexis is a crack shot.

BELOW One of Blake's greatest pleasures: shooting pool in the billiards room. Joseph had been his favorite competitor.

Alexis in the estate studio, 1981. The gifted Alexis is a critically acclaimed painter, but now that she is a businesswoman, she paints whenever she can to unwind.

Racing enthusiasts Blake and Krystle enjoy a day at the racetrack at Hollywood Park in Los Angeles, California. As a wedding present in 1983, Blake gave Krystle half ownership of a racehorse, Allegre. Peter de Vilbis owned the other half.

LEFT Alexis runs into Krystle at the jeweler's, much to their mutual dismay. The two women shop at many of the same stores, which is common for the very rich in Denver.

Tennis is as important to the Carringtons as polo is to Prince Charles. This is their time to relax, sharpen their reflexes, push themselves to their physical limits, and demonstrate their prowess as strategists. (All except Alexis, who refuses to perspire in public.) Here Krystle and Blake take on Fallon and Jeff in a weekend tennis game on the estate court. Krystle worked hard at improving her game; she *had* to. As she says, "Tennis is a blood sport out here. People have been executed for missing a backhand." Postgame is a time of unusual closeness for the Carringtons. The afternoon is usually rounded off with drinks, a rehash of the match, and loving laughter.

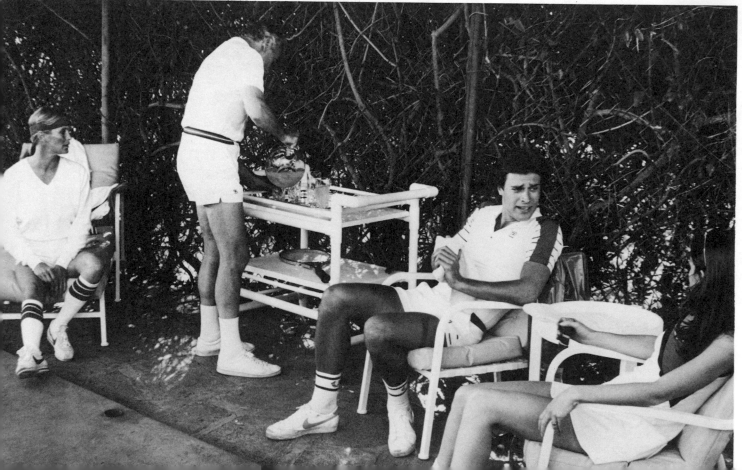

IV.
THE CARRINGTONS ON VIEW

BLAKE AND KRYSTLE'S FIRST WEDDING, 1980

On May 24, 1980, Blake Carrington took Krystle Jennings as his wife. The simple but elegant ceremony took place in the gilded ballroom of the Carrington mansion. The two hundred guests included Colorado's social, political, and business elite.

TOP LEFT The breathtakingly beautiful bride makes her way down the aisle.

LEFT Blake says, "I do."

RIGHT Mr. and Mrs. Blake Carrington.

An overview of the garden reception.

Steven, Fallon, and Blake, the small family unit for so many years.

Jeff with longtime Carrington family lawyer, Andrew Laird, and his uncle, Cecil Colby.

The cutting of the cake.

Getting ready to throw the bouquet.

The happy couple leaving the reception.

RIGHT AND BELOW As Krystle and Blake were leaving, Walter Lankershim crashed the reception to accuse Blake of trickery that threatened his oil leases. An ugly incident was barely averted.

At a crossroads concerning his sexuality, Steven regards the bouquet as a final irony to an exhausting day.

KRYSTLE'S FIRST BLACK-TIE DINNER PARTY AT HOME

K rystle's first dinner party for Blake's business associates and their wives, at the mansion, 1980, was strategic in gaining Blake much-needed financial support at that time of personal and professional crisis. Krystle was the perfect hostess, Fallon the less-than-perfect guest.

Just prior to the dinner party, Fallon lectured a very nervous Krystle: "My father is having people over on Saturday night. Important people. People who will either support him or turn their backs on him. The decisions will not be made on the balance in his checkbook. They will come in and they will look around, and very quietly they will judge whether Blake Carrington's table is brilliantly set. And whether his servants continue to respect him. And how well his wife and daughter are dressed. And from those things they will know the state of his mind . . . and the strength of his resolve."

The main entrée was a rack of lamb.

ABOVE LEFT Fallon had always been a social asset at Blake's dinner parties. Krystle's new role as hostess this night made her feel unneeded and restless.

ABOVE RIGHT The fashion press has described Krystle as "dressing just off-center enough to be sensational."

BELOW Blake and Cecil were amicable business rivals and best friends for over twenty-five years, but their relationship exploded dramatically in 1981.

In the course of the party, bored, feeling neglected, Fallon talked Jeff into smoking marijuana with her and going skinny-dipping in the pool. They were discovered.

Krystle and Blake enjoying an after-dinner brandy, agreeing that the evening went fairly smoothly, despite underlying tensions.

THE ROARING TWENTIES BALL: THE OPENING OF LA MIRAGE

In 1982, Fallon celebrated the opening of La Mirage by hostessing the infamous Roaring Twenties Ball. The highlight of the event was Fallon's show-stopping rendition of the Charleston on the pool diving board. She and hotel tennis pro Mark Jennings, who had joined her, made a splash in the society columns around the world.

The host and hostess, Mr. and Mrs. Marvin Davis.

Barbara Davis and Alexis Colby.

THE CAROUSEL BALL

The social event of the season in Denver is the annual Carousel Ball, held to raise money for the Children's Diabetes Foundation there.

Marvin Davis, the owner of Twentieth Century-Fox, and his lovely wife, Barbara, host this annual charity event. Nineteen eighty-three's special guests included President and Mrs. Gerald R. Ford and former Secretary of State Henry Kissinger. Blake and Alexis are generous contributors, and the Carringtons were there in full force to support the worthy cause.

Fallon, Blake, and Krystle.

ABOVE Dr. Henry A. Kissinger talks with the Honorable Gerald R. Ford.

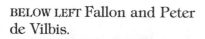

ABOVE Claudia and Steven.

BELOW LEFT Fallon and Peter de Vilbis.

BELOW RIGHT Mrs. Gerald (Betty) Ford being greeted by Barbara Davis.

BLAKE AND KRYSTLE'S "REAL" WEDDING, 1983

Having overcome many difficulties and much distress, Blake and Krystle were remarried in 1983. It was a glorious wedding, and this time *all* the Carrington children were home to witness their father's joy.

The ceremony reaffirming their vows was held in the living room of the mansion. A festive reception followed in the conservatory.

The happy couple enjoyed a romantic honeymoon at the Copacabana Playa Hotel in Rio de Janeiro.

LEFT Blake and Krystle receive congratulations from orchestra leader Peter Duchin, a close friend of Blake's who offered to play at the reception.

BELOW Blake and Krystle dance to "Embraceable You."

LEFT Fallon and Peter de Vilbis standing by the magnificent wedding feast.

BELOW LEFT Krystle made a secret wish before cutting the cake. She wished she could conceive another child. (The wish came true.)

BELOW RIGHT Adam, Steven, and Claudia. Any familial tension was put to rest this special day.

LITTLE BLAKE'S SECOND BIRTHDAY PARTY

In celebration of little Blake's second birthday in 1984, big Blake hosted the most lavish child's party in the history of Colorado. Jugglers, clowns, pony rides, carousel rides, balloons in profusion were featured, along with plenty of ice cream and cake for the diminutive guests. The extravaganza took place on the estate lawn.

LEFT Fallon once again can see the world with wondrous, innocent eyes through her son.

RIGHT Father Jeff as the happy clown—particularly since this day Fallon agreed to remarry him.

The proud grandparents with little Blake.

A group shot, full of fun, full of love.

Little Blake gets his first pony ride, with Blake, Krystle, and his nurse looking on.

ABOVE At least for the day, Claudia and Alexis patch things up between them for the sake of Steven, who took pictures.

RIGHT Steven and Alexis enjoying each other's company.

Blake and Krystle are hardly
average grandparents; they
are expecting a newborn
baby of their own.